FINDING Hope

CULTIVATING GOD'S GIFT OF A HOPEFUL SPIRIT

Marcia Ford

FOREWORD BY ANDREA JAEGER

Walking Together, Finding the Way®
SKYLIGHT PATHS® PUBLISHING
Woodstock, Vermont

Finding Hope:
Cultivating God's Gift of a Hopeful Spirit

2007 First Printing
© 2007 by Marcia Ford

For information regarding permission to reprint material from this book, please mail or fax your request in writing to SkyLight Paths Publishing, Permissions Department, at the address / fax number listed below, or e-mail your request to permissions@skylightpaths.com.

Library of Congress Cataloging-in-Publication Data
Ford, Marcia.
Finding hope : cultivating God's gift of a hopeful spirit / Marcia Ford.
p. cm.
"Walking together, finding the way".
Includes bibliographical references (p.   ).
ISBN-13: 978-1-59473-211-9 (quality pbk.)
ISBN-10: 1-59473-211-6 (quality pbk.)
1. Hope—Religious aspects—Christianity. 2. Hope—Religious aspects. 3. God. I. Title.

BV4638.F67 2006
234'.25—dc22

2006026319

10   9   8   7   6   5   4   3   2   1
Manufactured in Canada

SkyLight Paths Publishing is creating a place where people of different spiritual traditions come together for challenge and inspiration, a place where we can help each other understand the mystery that lies at the heart of our existence.

SkyLight Paths sees both believers and seekers as a community that increasingly transcends traditional boundaries of religion and denomination—people wanting to learn from each other, *walking together, finding the way.*

SkyLight Paths, "Walking Together, Finding the Way," and colophon are trademarks of LongHill Partners, Inc., registered in the U.S. Patent and Trademark Office.

Walking Together, Finding the Way
Published by SkyLight Paths Publishing
A Division of LongHill Partners, Inc.
Sunset Farm Offices, Route 4, P.O. Box 237
Woodstock, VT 05091
Tel: (802) 457-4000   Fax: (802) 457-4004
www.skylightpaths.com

To Fay Key and Steve Bullington
at Green Bough House of Prayer in Scott, Georgia.
You have given me hope that a better life is possible here and now,
in my daily routine, in my searching heart, in my uncertainty.
May God richly bless you for choosing lives of service, love, and devotion.
When I see you—when I simply think of you—I see God.

Contents

Contents

Foreword

Welcome to a wonderful blend of awe inspiring and down-home personal stories of hope from the famous to the people next door—and you. If you already possess hope, you will find ways to enrich the hope you have. If you can't seem to find the first steps to hope, you will find the essential fundamentals to get you started.

One of my favorite early stories of becoming aware of my need to ask for hope dates back to a time when I was on the professional tennis circuit and visited a local hospital's pediatric cancer ward. I was bringing gifts for the sick children, but it was the children with cancer and other diseases who gave me the gift of hope.

Through their simple, pure, and radiant ways, they let me know that their hope was also mine for the taking—if I wanted it. I didn't think I needed hope before I entered the hospital. I was feeling pretty good all around. I was healthy; I had the fame and fortune that came with being a teenage professional tennis player. I was feeling like Santa Claus. I expected to go back to the tournament with an empty sack and that was it.

But I went back with so much more. When I saw those kids playing, laughing, and appreciating every moment even before they received their gifts, I knew I wanted some of what they had. Despite not knowing if they would live to see their next birthdays, they possessed the gift of hope from God. That gift was transformed into an awareness and appreciation of life that allowed those children to sprinkle God's goodness on anyone that asked.

The hope those children gave me that day blossomed into a lifelong passion to build a better and brighter future filled with a lifetime of possibilities for children and their families. In pursuit of my own ability to inspire hope in others, I founded the Little

Star Foundation with fellow humanitarian Heidi Bookout. Together, we set out to change the world for children suffering from cancer and other diseases, neglect, and poverty. Little Star Foundation's programs have reached thousands of children, giving them and their families hope for the future. Through the work of Little Star, I've witnessed time and again the amazing strength that hope can bring. This gift continually restores my own reserves of hope and has changed my life forever.

In the pages that follow, you'll begin your own transformation to a life infused with hope. *Finding Hope* is for people interested in living a fuller life. We each have our own personal and unique journeys, yet there are some important constants that when followed allow individuals to embrace a life that is more fulfilling, enjoyable, and successful. In this book, Marcia Ford provides important learning tools that you can apply to your everyday life experiences. The transformations you can experience as you read this book will provide realistic solutions to deal with difficulties, pain, suffering, and secure the overall balance and peace you look to achieve in living the life God meant for you.

Through Marcia's extensive research and countless encounters of hope throughout the world you will discover that hope is for everyone. Hope is for those shooting for the stars, those trying to find some way to pick themselves up from despair, and for everyone in between. Hope reaches all races, religions, cultures, ages, and demographics. There is no goal so lofty, no pain so deep, no life so lost, no deed so dark, no sin so hideous that hope cannot penetrate to bring love, light, laughter, healing, and peace.

But hope requires an announcement that it is needed and wants to be found. An action must be established to get hope in motion. Searching for hope allows a person to have forward motion in the soulful awareness that there is more in life and that it is okay to pursue it. Faith tells us there is more to life than what our ordinary senses pick up. Hope is a combination, a bond of what we possess with what God possesses, and the culmination results in a faith—a life of hope—that is limitless.

This book makes sure you know that you are not alone in finding hope and that you are not too late. Life is a journey in process. God knows right where you are. The great thing about hope is that God knows actually how much to pour for you. God can pour an abundance so there is enough for you, with spillover to share with others. Or God can pour a small amount, encouraging you to return to God's hopeful filling station and bring others with you. God's filling station is never closed, always has plenty to go around, and is always free. All one has to do is ask to receive.

Our body, soul, spirit, mind, and heart have their own mechanisms to determine when hope is needed. When you encounter a need, simply announce, "I want some of that. Here I am. Fill me up, God."

So search for hope in the pages that follow, because they were written for you. The following stories of hope have the ability to infuse you with divine providence. Through God's gift of hope we can reach our potential as well as inspire, reach, connect with, and touch others. Hope is a powerful source of accomplishing what we were intended to accomplish.

As you make your way through this book, recognize that its effect on your life is just beginning. The blessings of this book will stay with you long after you've read the last words. The lessons enclosed are lifetime fruits that will allow you to go forth in life with much more than before you started reading this book. You may discover many more blessings as you allow hope to exist in your life—the way God intended.

Blessings,
Sister Andrea Cath Jaeger, OP
Cofounder, Little Star Foundation
Aspen, Colorado

Beginning with Hope

In his marvelous book *The Dark Night of the Soul,* a reflection on the writings of St. John of the Cross and Teresa of Ávila, Gerald May writes of being awestruck several times in his life by the power of what he calls "transformed hope." Transformed hope is that which has been through the fire and has emerged hotter, tougher, and more difficult to break. It's also a purified hope, free of contamination from extraneous materials that might keep it attached to the tangible—a particular dream for a particular outcome. It is simply hope, he writes, "naked hope, a bare energy of expectancy."[1]

One time and place where May discovered this naked hope was in the early 1990s in Bosnia during the three-year war that introduced the term "ethnic cleansing" to our everyday lexicon. There he met people who had nothing left—no families, no homes, no possessions. Nothing, that is, except the expressions of hope that May detected on their faces. He asked if that was true; did they really continue to have hope?

> "Yes, hope," they smiled.
> I asked if it was hope for peace.
> "No, things have gone too far for that."
> I asked if they hoped the United Nations or the United States would intervene in some positive way.
> "No, it is too late for that."

I asked them, "Then what is it you are hoping for?"

They were silent. They could not think of a thing to hope for, yet there it was—undeniable hope shining in them.

I asked one last question. "How can you hope, when there's nothing to hope for?"

The answer was ... the Serbo-Croatian word for God.[2]

That's it, really. Though we experience hope in a multitude of forms and manifestations, as people of faith our hope begins and ends with God. We may express our hope in more tangible ways; we hope for a particular job, an end to our pain and suffering, a restored relationship, peace on earth. Strip away those tangibles, though, and what you are left with is buck-naked hope. Our heart-pounding sense of expectancy finds its bare, raw energy in God. Our hope is God, and God is our hope.

Hope is so much like God that as we continue on our journey of faith, the two become indistinguishable. Like God, hope changes everything. When we come to know God, our lives are transformed; our eyes see the unseen, our ears hear the unspoken, our spirits sense the inexpressible. When we come to know hope, our lives are also transformed. We see the impossible made possible, we hear silent words of encouragement, we imagine the unimaginable.

Hope signifies God's covenant with us, the rainbow of promise that appears at just the right moment, when we look around and see nothing but devastation. Hope pushes back the waters that threaten to engulf us, as God's hands held back the waters of the Red Sea to give the children of Israel safe passage. Hope is God's healing touch, life-giving strength, resurrecting power. Hope revitalizes, refreshes, and rejuvenates us in body, mind, and spirit.

But before I lead you to believe that hope is just an abstract concept that showed itself in concrete image only in biblical times, let me say this: hope is a cat sitting by a

Dumpster in the dark of the night. I say this with absolute conviction. I know it to be true. When all hope was lost, Emily the Friendly Feline returned to my daughter's apartment complex several weeks after she escaped through a second-floor window. Emily had never known life in the wild; cuddled and coddled and cared for from day one, she had never even been outside on her own.

After three days of fruitless searching, calling, advertising, and contacting animal shelters within a thirty-mile radius, Elizabeth gave up hope of ever seeing her beloved Emily again. I believe we all did. My heart ached like crazy for my daughter.

But there Emily was, weeks later, sitting by the Dumpster as if she had been waiting impatiently for Elizabeth to finally get home from work that night. She made a show of running off, but Emily knows a good thing when she sees it, and that good thing was her caretaker. When Elizabeth called with the good and astonishing news, the word *miracle* actually crossed my husband's lips, perhaps for the first time in his life. This, he avowed, qualified for such a deviation from his normal linguistic behavior, which is to seldom say anything.

Many of us carry images of hope around with us. For Noah and his family, it was a rainbow shining through the clouds. For the Israelites fleeing Egypt, it was a wall of water on either side and dry ground underfoot. For the Ford family, it will always be a cat named Emily sitting by a Dumpster in the dark.

What are your personal images of hope? Whatever they are, carry them with you as you turn the pages that follow, where you'll likely discover more images to add to your collection. Together they will create a gallery of hope, a place where you can go to see the many evidences of hope in your life any time despair seeps in.

Let hope seep in instead. Let hope and faith and love and grace and all of those things that God is seep through the pores of your being until they fill you to overflowing. Another Gerald, Gerald Mann, believes that we can't build walls strong enough or thick enough or high enough to keep God's grace at bay:

> The seeping power of the message of Gods' grace is my hope. Grace means that the reality which is in, under, and above all things is gracious.... There's no stopping this message. It will seep through all of the walls we devise.[3]

God will give us the grace to keep our hope alive and flourishing. We just need to cooperate and accept the gift of grace—and the gift of hope.

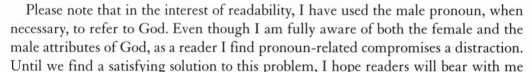

Please note that in the interest of readability, I have used the male pronoun, when necessary, to refer to God. Even though I am fully aware of both the female and the male attributes of God, as a reader I find pronoun-related compromises a distraction. Until we find a satisfying solution to this problem, I hope readers will bear with me with regard to this decision.

Hope is what sits by a window and waits for one more dawn, despite the fact that there isn't an ounce of proof in tonight's black, black sky that it can possibly come.

—**Joan Chittister**

Hope under Fire

1

Never deprive someone of hope; it might be all they have.
—Unknown

You've known them. I've known them. We've all known people who seem to work overtime at dashing our hopes. *Don't get your hopes up,* they say. *You know how you get—you're setting yourself up for a major disappointment.* Maybe. Maybe not. Either way, such unsolicited advice can drain the hope right out of us. But we can't let that happen; we need instead to learn how to hold on with everything we've got to the measure of hope we have. Even when we suspect the naysayers are right.

Of all people, I should be the most wary of getting my hopes up. As a child, I pretty much sabotaged Christmas by getting sick to my stomach every Christmas Eve. It wasn't because I had high hopes of getting a lot of wonderful gifts or even of getting one particular gift, such as "an official Red Ryder carbine action two-hundred shot range model air rifle with a compass in the stock and this thing which tells time." (If you don't understand this reference, watch Jean Shepherd's *A Christmas Story*—one of my all-time favorite movies and a Ford-family

Hope is readily available to all of us, even in the midst of tragedy. And not only hope for eternal life and hope of being reunited with those we love. Hope is available right now, square in the middle of tragedy, because God has promised to walk with us through any disaster that might overtake us.

—LUIS PALAU

holiday tradition.) It was the sheer excitement of the holiday, the anxious hope that this one day would be different from every other day of the year. I can remember praying—literally praying—that I would not die before Christmas. I prayed that prayer every year throughout my childhood, starting in early December.

Christmas always came, of course, and I didn't die even once, so every year my hopes were realized. But still. If your hopes are so inflated that they make you ill, something's got to change.

For me, I'm guessing they never will. Though I've become a master at hiding it, I continue to entertain high hopes about life, despite any and all evidence to the contrary. I'm so good at hiding it that some people consider me cynical at times. But my identity as a cynic simply serves to mask my true identity, that of—dare I even say it?—a hopeful optimist. The mask is a perennial defense against those who would try to burst every jubilant bubble that rises to the surface of my life.

Maybe you know what I mean. Maybe you've been called naïve, gullible, ignorant about life, or a Pollyanna, all because you choose hope over despair (which is different from choosing hope over reality, by the way).

So what do we do about the naysayers? You harbor the hope deep within you that your cheating partner will recognize the value of faithfulness. You hope and pray that your overtime check will cover the increase in rent this month. You want to believe that multiple doctors are wrong—your mother's cancer is not terminal. But the critics won't shut up. Even when they're not around, you hear them. *He'll never give up those other women.* Or *See? I told you you're heading for eviction!* Or *You should have known she wouldn't get any better.*

And then your worst fears are realized. Your critics are proven right—and they're right about things far more serious than holidays. Your philandering partner leaves you—for your best friend. You don't have enough money for the rent—which is now overdue. Your mother dies—even sooner than expected.

This is where the rubber meets the road—where our critics create the friction that reveals our underlying philosophy of hope. On the surface, we by all means do hope that the one we love will always be faithful and that our financial needs will always be met and that the significant people in our lives will always be around. The surface, however, is the part that's exposed to our detractors and is the area of our lives where we're most vulnerable. Much deeper is where our true feelings about hope lie.

It's possible, I suppose, that your true feelings about hope mirror your surface hopes—in other words, the only real hope you have in life is that certain things will always turn out in your favor—but I trust that's not the case. I trust you've found something to place your hope in other than the uncertainty and unpredictability of life on Earth.

I hope that "something" is God. Because when your ultimate hope is in God, your underlying philosophy of hope is based on the unshakeable belief that no matter what happens, God will see you through it. And when you hold on to that belief deep down inside of you, the people who threaten to rob you of your

> Beware how you take away hope from another human being.
> —**OLIVER WENDELL HOLMES**

When God wanted to guarantee his promises, he gave his word, a rock-solid guarantee—God can't break his word. And because his word cannot change, the promise is likewise unchangeable. It's an unbreakable spiritual lifeline, reaching past all appearances right to the very presence of God.

—HEBREWS 6:17–19

(*THE MESSAGE*)

hope cannot—simply cannot—have any power over you, nor can they touch the hope that lies within you.

Untouchable hope. That's what we all need. A hope that is steadfast and sure and protected from every effort to destroy it. And that's the kind of hope we need to share with those people who have lost the hope they once had, either because they placed their hope in their circumstances or because they allowed someone to deprive them of what little hope they had.

Cultivating a "no matter what" approach to our faith in God creates that untouchable kind of hope. When we have an untouchable faith, then no matter what happens, we believe God will be with us. No matter what, we believe God loves us. No matter what, we believe God will see us through. Just let someone try to take that away from us.

REFLECTION

Is your faith in God untouchable? If you're not sure, give some thought to how you could strengthen your faith—and to what is keeping you from a "no matter what" faith. We don't know how strong our faith is until it's tested; we need to nurture it and tend to it so it will be able to withstand the pressures and strains and stresses of life. Our hope is so closely tied to our faith that at times the two are indistinguishable. Strengthening our faith can't help but build up our hope; an unshakeable faith produces unquenchable hope.

PRACTICE

Deeply embedded in our memory banks are the countless responses we've received to every hopeful thought we've uttered. Some encouraged our hope; some jeopardized our hope; some may have completely shut down our hope. As these memories come to mind—and they will as you continue to read about hope—begin to formulate appropriate, and gracious, responses to people who challenge your hope. This is not only practical but also scriptural; 1 Peter 3:15 advises the followers of Jesus to "always be prepared to give an answer to everyone who asks you to give the reason for the hope that you have. But do this with gentleness and respect" (NIV).

The gift we can offer others is so simple a thing as hope.

—DANIEL BERRIGAN

2 Dealing with Disappointment

We must accept finite disappointment, but we must
never lose infinite hope.

—Martin Luther King Jr.

One of the most puzzling verses in the Christian Scriptures
assures us—or tries to assure us—that "hope does not disappoint" (Rom. 5:5, NKJV). What on earth are we to make of
that? Haven't we all had our hopes disappointed? I know people who have become embittered toward God when time after
time their hopes went unfulfilled. Their once-vibrant faith
dwindled and eventually died.

That's not all the verse says, though; it continues with what
appears to be an explanation: "because the love of God has been
poured out in our hearts by the Holy Spirit who was given to
us." The logic is this: God gave us the Spirit, who poured God's
love into our hearts, and therefore hope doesn't disappoint.
Hmm ... I think we need to look beyond logic to figure this
one out, because logic isn't enough to explain what Paul meant
in this verse.

For a deeper explanation of the kind of hope Paul
wrote about, I'll turn our attention to Beth Stroud, a United

Methodist pastor in Philadelphia. This is what she had to say in a 2005 sermon about the kind of hope God gives us:

> What kind of hope shall we have? Not hope in a certain outcome from a particular event taking place at one moment in time.... That isn't really hope; that's more of a test. It's asking for proof that God is with us, rather than taking the risk of commitment to a better future God has in mind even though we can't see it now.... [Hope in a certain outcome] is probably closer to despair in some ways than it is to hope; it means you've almost given up already, and you're just waiting for the last straw.
>
> But the hope God gives us is a hope in a larger unfolding of grace and goodness transcending the immediate present. The hope God gives us is a deep confidence that the whole world is held in loving and compassionate hands, and that even the things that go so terribly wrong are being transformed into instruments of healing and justice.[4]

That, I think, encapsulates the problem many of us have with hope. We have hope in a certain outcome rather than hope in a "larger unfolding of grace and goodness," one that extends beyond our immediate circumstances and points to a future in God that will not disappoint. Stroud's interpretation clearly describes that unfolding as taking place in this life. God is holding the world in loving and compassionate hands today,

> Now hope does not disappoint, because the love of God has been poured out in our hearts by the Holy Spirit who was given to us.
>
> —ROMANS 5:5 (NKJV)

right now. We won't have to wait for the afterlife to see the transformation of so many things that have gone so terribly wrong.

If we look carefully enough into our own lives, we should be able to discover moments when an event that brought us great pain actually resulted in healing or justice. Many a divorced woman or man can relate to that concept. The immediate circumstances surrounding the death of a marriage are often painful, humiliating, and seemingly hopeless. The spouse who feels especially wronged is the one most likely to hope for a particular outcome, such as the restoration of the marriage or the quick demise of the offending mate. That, to me, illustrates Stroud's description of a kind of hope that is closer to despair; the offended mate closes off every possibility other than the one he or she is focused on, and that's a setup for disappointment.

Meanwhile, God is setting the stage for an unfolding of grace and goodness that is hard to see when your heart has been shattered. Some people never do see it. God, or life, has disappointed them. Their hopes for the future have evaporated. The love of their life is gone. And they spend the rest of their lives in bitterness and despair. The stage God has set for them remains bare; there's no one to experience the grace and goodness that could be theirs, because those who hold on to bitterness are blind to the larger vision God has for their lives.

"We must accept finite disappointment," Martin Luther King Jr. said, "but we must never lose infinite hope." King certainly hoped for particular outcomes in the civil rights move-

> The just have entrusted their cause to the Lord, who does not remain indifferent to their imploring eyes, who does not ignore their plea, who does not disappoint their hope.
>
> —POPE BENEDICT XVI

ment, but he was wise enough not to pin his hopes on seeing those outcomes realized in his lifetime. Despite one setback after another, he never stopped believing that, ultimately, his hope would not be disappointed. He had infinite hope—the hope that one day, God would right the many wrongs King had witnessed and experienced as a leader in the fight for desegregation, voting rights for blacks, and basic human rights. Though progress has been made, that day still has not come. I can't help but believe that had King lived, he would have continued working, believing, and hoping for the day when God would transform injustice into an instrument of healing.

Our disappointment is finite; our hope must not be. Dwelling on disappointed hopes erodes our faith in the Spirit, who poured God's love into our hearts. What a waste of love it would be if we expended our spiritual energy in testing God with a specific set of outcomes! That's like trying to work out a back-room deal with God: *If you make my partner come back to me, restore our marriage, and take away all my disappointment, then I'll still believe in you.* No matter how things end up, that's a lose-lose proposition for you. If your partner fails to return, you've lost your relationship with God; if the marriage is restored, your faith in God will be resting on a shaky foundation.

We need to fasten our hopes to the one sure thing in life— God. God is infinite, and the hope God gives us is infinite. Times of disappointment—some more traumatic and severe than others—will occur throughout our lifetime. Our response during those times depends on where we've placed our hope.

> If we will be quiet and ready enough, we shall find compensation in every disappointment.
> —HENRY DAVID THOREAU

REFLECTION

Susanna Wesley knew disappointment. The mother of Methodist leaders John and Charles Wesley, she witnessed the deaths of ten of her nineteen children; another child was permanently maimed in an accident. Her tyrannical husband, a pastor, caused the family severe financial problems and abandoned her and their children for a full year after a minor squabble. Twice the homes they were living in burned to the ground. And yet she continued to believe in God's ability to transform her "disappointments and calamities" into a higher purpose:

> Help me, O Lord, to make a true use of all disappointments and calamities in this life, in such a way that they may unite my heart more closely with you. Cause them to separate my affections from worldly things and inspire my soul with more vigor in the pursuit of true happiness.[5]

Susanna Wesley's desire to "separate [her] affections from worldly things" seems archaic to contemporary ears, and yet sometimes our disappointment does result from too great an affection for things—consumer goods. But when it comes to the significant disappointments in life, your faith and your hope is on the line. Do you believe God can transform your times of disappointment? Do you believe those times can be used to unite your heart more closely to God?

Trials, temptations, disappointments—all these are helps instead of hindrances, if one uses them rightly. They not only test the fiber of character but strengthen it.

—JAMES BUCKHAM

PRACTICE

It's not just the people in our lives who disappoint us. Sometimes it's God—or so it appears. If you believe God has disappointed you in some way, vent your frustration. Holding back our feelings of disappointment, whether they are with God or with another human being, hurts us immeasurably. When we fail to deal with our disappointment, we allow it to fester and grow into bitterness and anger—two emotions we do not want to harbor in our soul. In all the times I have gotten real with God about my disappointment in him, not once have I sensed a shred of judgment—just acceptance and kindness. I was more judgmental of my ranting and railing than God was. One more thing: when you're done venting, ask God to show you how your disappointment can help to strengthen and transform your character, as well as toughen you up for the inevitability of future disappointments.

3

It's Not Wishful Thinking

Hope is not the conviction that something will turn out
well, but the certainty that something makes sense
regardless of how it turns out.

—Václav Havel

Hope is such an ethereal concept that people often resort to
using inadequate synonyms—words like "dream" or "desire"
or "wish"—to describe what it is. None of those words is sufficient, least of all "wish." Yet "wish" is a word so closely linked
to hope that some people accuse those of us who are hopeful of
being victims of wishful thinking.

Let me speak on behalf of all my fellow hopeful spirits and
say that we are decidedly not victims. At least, we are not victims of wishful thinking. And here's my defense: wishful
thinking is rooted in fantasy; hope is rooted in wisdom.

One of the clearest ways to get a handle on the distinction
between wishful thinking and genuine hope is to look at one
area of life that affects the vast majority of the population, our
day-to-day finances. (Here, "finances"—a rather lofty term,
don't you think?—is something of a euphemism for our very
daily need of not-so-daily money.) When you dig deeper into
the way people think, you learn that those who indulge in

money-oriented wishful thinking lead a fairly scary fantasy life. Big money is always just around the bend: They're next up to win both the Powerball and the Mega Millions lottery. The Publishers Clearinghouse Prize Patrol is on its way to their doorstep. Bill Gates needs to dispose of another million or so, and they're his new favorite charity.

Those whose fantasies are a bit less scary still see some kind of bailout on the horizon. A few of the single parents I know keep thinking that they're destined to meet someone who will rescue them and their children by providing a comfortable living for them. And if I could stomach watching the local news, I'm guessing that at least once or twice a week I'd see a story about an area resident who was scammed out of a whole lot of money because they believed some get-rich-quick scheme. (I live in central Florida, close to Orlando. Living as close as we do to the wonderful world of Disney, it's amazing that Orlandoans don't fall prey to those magical promises more often than we do.)

Believe me, wishful thinkers are the real victims here.

It's not that the big money and the big bailouts don't exist. Some people really do win multimillion-dollar lotteries and sweepstakes prizes, or so I've heard. Mr. or Ms. Right does occasionally come with an impressive financial portfolio. Some people really do get rich quick. It's just that those things happen to so few people, and all those wishful thinkers have no substantial basis for hoping that they'll be among that select few.

Hope, by contrast, has a firm foundation. Hebrews 11:1 says this: "Now faith is the substance of things hoped for, the evidence of things not seen" (KJV). We'll come across this verse

What can be hoped for which is not believed?

—St. Augustine

13

from the Christian Scriptures again, but here it's important to notice the word "substance." I believe the writer of Hebrews is making a two-pronged point here; just like our English word, the Greek word for "substance"—*hupostasis,* if you must know—carries a dual meaning. It can refer to something that has a foundation and to something with a substantial quality. Both describe the hope we have in God. Our faith helps us to see the unseen—the things of God that are invisible to our physical eyes but visible to our spiritual eyes—and our hope is built upon the substantial foundation of the promises of God.

That's all well and good, but the bills still have to be paid. So how do we who have this lovely concept of hope wafting about on some otherworldly level believe we will get the wretched money we need to pay all those ungodly bills for the rest of our lives? I suppose we could be like the woman who once wrote a $700,000 check to *The 700 Club* because she believed God was going to make a miraculous deposit in her very empty checking account. (God didn't, in case you're curious.) Religious wishful thinkers are just as deceived as their secular counterparts—or more so, since they really ought to know better.

Our hope needs to be grounded in spiritual reality—the reality that whether God provides that constantly changing amount of money we need *right now,* the Spirit of God will see us through our times of want and need. I'm convinced that kind of hope only flourishes in a heart that is open to wisdom beyond human understanding. I base that conviction on decades of personal experience and observation. Countless times in my life I experienced a deep inner knowing that we would make it

Hope is the belief, more or less strong, that joy will come.

—Sydney Smith

through a financial crisis (there I go with another euphemism—we were broke). Sometimes unexpected money came in, but more often than not we simply had to tough it out and cope with the consequences.

What sets people of hope apart is not only how they bear up under adverse circumstances but also how they view the future in light of past and present circumstances. Maybe God has never come through with an unexpected check in the past, and maybe God didn't come through with an unexpected check this time either, but wisdom teaches us that our hope does not lie in one specific solution to our problems. It lies in a God who has blessed us with an inordinate measure of grace and resilience and endurance, and who has embedded in our every experience the insight and wisdom we need to help others find the hope that infuses our lives.

Are we victims of wishful thinking? I think not.

REFLECTION

Like hope, wisdom is a concept that's hard to define. We can come up with a dictionary definition if we have to, but it's easier to recognize when we see it than to define by using words. What, in your experience, is wisdom? Where do you see evidences of it in your life? Do you catch glimpses of wisdom in conversations with friends and loved ones, sermons you hear, books you read, media you listen to or watch—or in your own thoughts? Think about the relationship between hope and wisdom. The Christian Bible tells us to be "wise as serpents and

> Trust in the Lord with all your heart, and lean not on your own understanding; in all your ways acknowledge Him, and He will direct your paths.
>
> **—PROVERBS 3:5–6**
> **(NKJV)**

15

innocent as doves" (Matt. 10:16, NRSV); is it possible to be as wise as a serpent and not become cynical rather than hopeful?

PRACTICE

The biblical book of Proverbs contains a wealth of wisdom. One of the most long-lasting, beneficial spiritual practices I have followed in my life is the practice of reading a chapter of the book of Proverbs each day. It's one of the easiest reading plans to follow; since there are thirty-one chapters in Proverbs, you simply read the chapter that corresponds with the day's date, doubling up on the last day or days when the month has fewer than thirty-one days. To make your reading especially effective, switch translations every few months. That's easier to do than ever, now that so many version of the Bible are available in their entirety on Internet sites such as www.cross-walk.com and www.biblegateway.com.

Let us live like people who see the invisible, who are animated by the Spirit of God.

—WRITINGS OF THE CARTHUSIAN MONKS

Postmodern Vision 4

If you want to build a ship, don't herd people together to collect wood and don't assign them tasks and work, but rather teach them to long for the endless immensity of the sea.
—Antoine de Saint-Exupéry

After years of exposure to the thinking of a wide assortment of kids in the Millennial Generation (children born between approximately 1977 and 1995, formerly described as Generation Y), I've come to an astonishing conclusion about the parents of today's teenagers and young adults: we somehow managed to carefully, conscientiously, and at times neurotically rear our offspring without ever passing along to them anything resembling a meaningful understanding of the concept of hope. I'm dead serious about that. Before you take me to task on that assertion, hear me out.

First of all, I realize that every generation has produced its share of hopeless kids—teenagers who rebelled and dropped out of school and ended up living a just-getting-by existence. Those aren't the kids I'm talking about.

I also realize that every generation has produced its share of kids who despaired of life itself, who suffered mental and emotional problems so severe that they could not live a normal existence. Those also aren't the kids I'm talking about.

Finally, I realize that the generation that parented the kids who do not seem to comprehend the notion of hope is not entirely to blame. I'm one of those parents, and I can assure you, I'm not about to place all that blame on myself. I have this nagging feeling, though, that while we were being so careful, so conscientious, and so neurotic about rearing our offspring, our kids were happily going about their lives and subconsciously picking up the vibes of a seismic shift taking place in our culture. They were closer to the ground, after all, at least when they were younger. It's no wonder they could sense tremors that didn't even register on our personal Richter scales.

The shift I allude to is the transition from a modern to a postmodern culture. I could, and someday may, write a book about all the ways postmodernism has changed the children we so carefully nurtured. But for now, I'm focused on hope, and here's the thing that is vexing about so many Millennials: they experience neither hope nor despair. They see life as ultimately absurd, but that neither bothers them nor inspires them to try to make some sense of it all. Life just is what it is. They're not interested in the just-getting-by existence of the rebels, but neither do they aspire to greatness with regard to the impact their life's work can have on the world. I don't mean they fail to strive for excellence; they simply wouldn't describe it in that way. They do what they love, they love what they do, and that produces ... excellence. But that's not a word they would use. Their

Sanity may be madness but the maddest of all is to see life as it is and not as it should be.

—FROM *DON QUIXOTE DE LA MANCHA*

work is just what it is. If they're happy with it, cool. If their work can bring some pleasure to other people, also cool. If not, cool anyway.

When some Millennials ask, "What's the use?"—which they do, with a frequency that would seem to be cause for alarm, but isn't—they really *are* just asking a rhetorical question. They're not expressing despair or hopelessness; they don't want or need an answer; they're not sending a hidden message that they're packing it in and giving up on life. Still, when it comes to hope, they just don't get it.

Here's my proposal for correcting our oversight, our failure to impart to Millennials an understanding of the concept of hope: give them a "vision" of hope. Millennials love visions, just as they love stories. Combine a vision with a story, and you've hooked them. Antoine de Saint-Exupéry, an author who lived in the first half of the twentieth century, would have felt right at home with today's young people and probably could have taught us a thing or two about how best to convey hope through visions and stories. Don't distribute shipbuilding materials and assign tasks, he would say. Give people a vision of the vast, endless sea, and the job is as good as done. Expose a pile of rocks not for what it is but for what it could be, and a cathedral is as good as built. That's Millennial thinking.

I'm not suggesting this is going to be easy; I think even Monsieur Saint-Exupéry would face a challenge or two in communicating hope to a generation that accepts life for what it is rather than having a vision for what it could be. But this is our legacy that we're talking about here (don't get me started on

> A rock pile ceases to be a rock pile the moment a single man contemplates it, bearing within him the image of a cathedral.
>
> —ANTOINE DE SAINT-EXUPÉRY

19

their inability to understand or care about a legacy, whether it's ours or theirs).

If the concept of hope is all that important to us—and if you've read this far, I'm guessing it's all that important to you—then we need to find creative ways to pass a legacy of hope along to those who come after us. We can start by living in a way that is consistent with the hope we profess. It's important that we model hope, but we need to do more. We need to seek God's wisdom and God's understanding of how Millennials think, and then tap into the creative Spirit of God to discover the images and metaphors and stories that resonate with them so we can communicate hope to them. If our first attempts appear to work, cool. If they don't, not so cool. But we still have our own hope, and our own hope will strengthen our resolve to get the job done.

REFLECTION

What images and metaphors convey the concept of hope to you? An example would be the first crocus or forsythia bush in spring. Or Emily Dickinson's classic poem, "Hope Is the Thing with Feathers":

> *Hope is the thing with feathers*
> *That perches in the soul,*
> *And sings the tune without the words,*
> *And never stops at all,*

Our imagination is the only limit to what we can hope to have in the future.

—CHARLES F. KETTERING

And sweetest in the gale is heard;
And sore must be the storm
That could abash the little bird
That kept so many warm.
I've heard it in the chillest land,
And on the strangest sea;
Yet, never, in extremity,
It asked a crumb of me.

Not my cup of poetic tea, but it gets the point across. As you think about the images that come to mind as you ruminate on the concept of hope, ask yourself if those same images would resonate with teenagers or twentysomethings. (I'm guessing "the thing with feathers" wouldn't, but maybe I'm just a Dickinson cynic.) Then try to come up with a metaphor that would speak to those age groups ("Hope is the thing that stores 7,500 digital songs in a cell phone–sized case ..." is *not* the way to start).

PRACTICE

In early 2006, a groundbreaking interfaith meeting went nearly unnoticed by the media, including journalists who cover religion. The meeting brought together two elements of post-modern faith, one Jewish, known as Synagogue 3000, (www.synagogue3000.org), and one Christian, known as Emergent/U.S. (www.emergentvillage.org). Leaders of the two

You are not here merely to make a living. You are here in order to enable the world to live more amply, with greater vision, with a finer spirit of hope and achievement. You are here to enrich the world, and you impoverish yourself if you forget the errand.

—WOODROW T. WILSON

movements shared their thoughts on building spiritual communities in today's religious climate. If you're not familiar with what is known as emergent faith—and if you want to discover how to relate to and minister to postmoderns—then step one is to visit these websites. The ideas coming out of the emerging church movement are more exciting than anything that's come down the pike since the Jesus Movement. And author Rabbi Larry Hoffman, a leader in the movement to "reinvent the synagogue," says there's evidence of emerging forms of congregational life in Jewish congregations as well.

Step two: Attend a postmodern, emergent-type worship service if you can find one. A good place to start for Christian services is Ginkworld.net, which features links to hundreds of churches grouped geographically (www.ginkworld .net/churches/churchesmain.html). Or look around for "churches"—they often meet in warehouses, coffee shops, art galleries, music studios, and the like—with offbeat names: Mosaic, Edge, Paradox, Epic, Quest, Flood/H^{2}O, and my favorite, Scum of the Earth (they're in Denver, just so you know). To find synagogues, www.synagogue3000.org lists rabbis and congregations affiliated with the Jewish emergent movement. One more thing: emergent is often referred to as a movement among Gen Xers and Millennials, but don't let that discourage you if you're older. I'm totally at home in the emerging church, and I'm a certified Boomer—as is Brian McLaren, the undisputed leader of the emerging church movement.

Impossible Situations

Hope sees the invisible, feels the intangible, and achieves the impossible.

—Charles Caleb Colton[6]

Hanging out with Millennials can be a dizzying experience. The generation that turned the word "whatever" into a philosophy of life is the same generation that may very well trash the word "impossible." "Whatever" implies that whatever happens just happens; it doesn't matter, it has no meaning, it makes no difference. That attitude, though, bears little resemblance to the way Millennials perceive reality. Theirs is an "everything is possible" reality. You say pigs can't fly? Of course they can.

It's hard to keep your bearings as you watch the contradictions go ping-ponging through Millennials' lives. What makes it so maddening is that you're there struggling to maintain your equilibrium in their incongruous world while they nonchalantly walk right by you, totally at home in a paradoxical environment.

Really, though, those of us who are older should be the ones to trash the concept of impossibility. Millennials have no

Jesus looked at them intently and said, "Humanly speaking, it is impossible. But with God everything is possible."

—MATTHEW 19:26
(NLT)

problem believing in the impossible because all they've known is an abundance of possibilities, especially with regard to technology. The rest of us, however, once functioned on a daily basis without the benefit of a personal computer and actually lived to tell about it. We should be the first to believe that nothing is truly impossible. And what's more, we ought to be applauded for that belief because we came by it honestly. We've seen the impossible become a reality. So why do we have such a hard time believing that impossible situations can be turned around?

One reason is that we, as an oh-so-advanced culture, think we're so smart. We may grudgingly admit that we cannot fathom where technology will ultimately take us, but aside from that one itty-bitty concession, we seem to have reached the conclusion that we're about as civilized and knowledgeable and clever as any society will ever be. (Future societies will likely use the word *delusional* to characterize us.)

Unfortunately, this faulty way of thinking carries over to difficulties in our everyday lives. We *know* that people don't change. We *know* that a diagnosis of terminal cancer is a death sentence. We *know* that criminals can't be rehabilitated. We *know,* we *know,* we *know.* And so the impossibilities in life remain impossible.

A second reason we have such a hard time believing the impossible is that we consider that way of thinking equivalent to living in denial. But those two concepts are not the same thing at all. In fact, for people who profess faith in God, the very opposite is true: refusing to believe that all things are possible is living in denial of their profession of faith. If you believe in a powerful God (who would bother to believe in a powerless God, I wonder?), then I don't think you have much choice but to believe that God can do the impossible.

The late actor Christopher Reeve, who was paralyzed in a horseback-riding accident, was hardly living in denial when he expressed his belief that paralysis could be cured; rather, he was believing the impossible from the confines of his very real wheelchair. Likewise, Michael J. Fox, actor turned medical research advocate, does not deny that he has Parkinson's disease—an exceedingly difficult disorder to treat, with no cure in sight—when he confidently asserts, "The war against Parkinson's is winnable."[7] Believing the impossible is not denying reality; it's believing that God can intervene in reality and change it for the better.

Another reason we continue to call situations impossible is that we ignore the all-important factor of time. What appears to be impossible today may be entirely possible a year from now.

A year before we bought our first house, I did not believe we would ever be in a position to own a home. I come from a family of renters, and I carried that tenant mentality with me for years. Home ownership took on a nearly mythical quality for me; its pathway was shrouded in secrecy, and only a privileged segment of society could find the way through the mist. Okay, so maybe I had a flair for the dramatic, but really, I never thought I'd be a homeowner.

And then one day we received a letter—yes, a letter; it was that long ago—from our landlord. She had decided to sell the

I have learned to use the word *impossible* with the greatest caution.

—WERNHER VON BRAUN

25

house and was offering it to us for under market value because we had been good tenants. Everything changed the moment I read that letter, and yet, nothing had changed. Our income and circumstances were exactly the same, but I *knew* the house was as good as ours. Well, one thing had changed—my attitude. That letter gave me hope, even though there was no earthly reason why it should have; after all, "under market value" was still way out of reach for us.

Nothing extraordinary happened in the months after we received that letter—no major windfall or inheritance—just a series of unremarkable and unlikely events that worked together to make it possible for us to buy the house. Over time, the impossible became possible.

If I shared that story with my Millennial friends—especially if I added all the energy and excitement and colorful details that I'm sparing you—they would probably ask, "And?" wondering when I was going to get to the good part. And then they'd just shrug it off as another lame story told by an eccentric Boomer. Whatever.

I'm glad they're jaded on impossibilities. When you have no idea that something can't be done, it's amazing how quickly you can do it.

REFLECTION

Nearly everyone has a story about a time in their lives when something that seemed impossible actually came to pass. Think

Jesus said to him, "If you can believe, all things are possible to him who believes." Immediately the father of the child cried out and said with tears, "Lord, I believe; help my unbelief!"

—MARK 9:23–24

(NKJV)

about one such time in your life. Why did you think the situation was impossible? When did you realize that the situation could change? What made the difference? Give the same careful thought to an impossible situation in your life today.

PRACTICE

A theology class that I mentor once got into a lively and, at times, heated discussion about slavery at the time of Jesus. Some members of the class could not fathom how the Romans, and later on, the early Christians, could not know that slavery was wrong. Others suggested they try to imagine a culture that had no idea how else to get menial jobs done. The discussion reached an impasse when those in the first group insisted that the time in which a condition exists is of no consequence. If we know slavery is wrong today, then the Romans and Christians knew it then, and they should have eliminated it. I decided it was time to play "What If?" I suggested we take a fact of everyday life that no one questions—the example I used was the incarceration of convicted criminals—and fast-forward to a time when people will believe that it's a no-brainer to consider incarceration wrong. How would that future civilization handle lawbreakers?

Exercises like that one shake the cobwebs out of our brains. Think of something in your life that you take for granted—something you would like to change but cannot see any way it could be changed. Then imagine a future world in which such

> We have a God who delights in impossibilities.
> —ANDREW MURRAY

27

a change is possible. What is different about that world compared to the world you live in today? What could you do—if you shook the cobwebs out of your brain—to move closer to that future world of greater possibilities?

Recovering from Loss

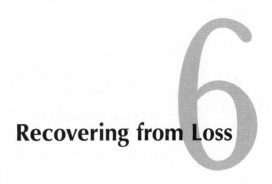

Hope is grief's best music.

—Author Unknown

At a recent training session for hospice volunteers, the focus turned to ways we can offer our patients a certain measure of control over their remaining days on Earth. One volunteer, whose wisdom I had come to appreciate in other meetings, contributed this thought: "As we get older, life becomes a series of little give-ups. After a while, we can't help but become discouraged." He was speaking of healthy people, or at least not those under hospice care—people like me, who have had to give up all manner of food and drink and addictions until it seems that the only choice we have left is an ounce of fat-free cottage cheese. But we all got his point: people who are dying experience an accelerated degree of give-ups, and we need to give back to them whatever control is appropriate in order to help them compensate for what they have lost.

Losses, of course, come in all shapes and sizes. What may be a significant loss to you may bewilder me to no end. But there are some losses that I think we can all agree are fairly

When we come into the present, we begin to feel the life around us again, but we also encounter whatever we have been avoiding. We must have the courage to face whatever is present—our pain, our desires, our grief, our loss, our secret hopes, our love—everything that moves us most deeply.

—JACK KORNFIELD

traumatic: losing a loved one to death or divorce or a breakup; losing a job; losing a home or possessions due to a natural disaster, financial ruin, or criminal activity. There are others that are less tangible but equally traumatic, such as losing our sense of safety and security as a result of a catastrophic event in our lives.

In our recent shared history, there's no better example of the impact of loss than the devastation caused by Hurricane Katrina. How on earth do you recover from that? I don't mean physically; people can be exceedingly resourceful when they need to be. I mean emotionally and spiritually. It seems impossible that some Katrina victims have kept from losing all their marbles along with their security, their possessions, and sometimes even their families. And yet, they have.

Our diocese in Florida is among hundreds across the country that regularly sends volunteers and supplies to the Gulf Coast to help in the rebuilding effort. The stories the volunteers tell when they return contain a handful of common elements: courage, determination, faith, and, yes, hope. But the kind of hope they witness in Mississippi and Louisiana is remarkable in that it's a hope *that has already faced loss.* In many other situations, people have hope that either something good will happen or something bad won't happen. But for Katrina victims, the bad has already happened. The storm's victims have no hope that friends or relatives who lost their lives will miraculously come back to life. They have no hope that their homes and cars and possessions—and jobs—will suddenly be restored, as if nothing ever happened. And they have no hope that their lives will ever be the same.

So what are these hopeful victims pinning their hope on? Their loved ones will never return, but they can still cherish the memories they have of those who died, memories that no one can ever take away from them. Their tangible property is gone, but they can still have a vision for the future—even if it is a radically different scenario from the way they lived in the past. Their lives will never be the same, but maybe, just maybe, that's not such a bad thing. Hopeful people have an amazing ability to believe that "all things work together for good" (Rom. 8:28, NRSV) without in any way minimizing the devastating effect of the losses they've suffered.

People who have suffered loss often learn to hold on lightly to what they have because they've experienced the reality of losing loved ones and possessions and opportunities in a heartbeat. The trick comes in having the right attitude toward the loss they've suffered—a trick I've yet to master. When I was five— that's right, many, many decades ago—I gave my little heart and soul to a puppy named Buttons. Buttons, however, died when he was hit by a car shortly after we got him. That did it for me. I ignored every pet my family acquired after Buttons, and even today, the various pets we've had as the Ford family have all belonged to the children—never to me. I probably need major therapy, but there it is. I hold on lightly to pets, because pets die. Other, more sensible people who have lost pets have learned the fine art of loving a new pet *despite* the fact that it could die. That, I'm sure, is the right attitude to have.

We walk a fine line here on Earth, don't we? We want—and *should* want—to partake of all that life has to offer, to be

> Saying goodbye to a loved one is not the same as forgetting them or ceasing to think about them. It is simply the way of owning the loss, integrating it, accepting its restrictions and limitations and saying yes to life without the one who has died.
>
> —JOYCE HUGGETT

anchored in the here and now with everything that brings us joy. And yet, we have another attachment—a feeling that we are not of this world, that there is another life beyond this one that will require us to either gradually let go of those things that tie us to Earth or to make a clean break of it. It's been said that the losses we suffer, even those that weigh us down with grief so profound we believe we will not survive it, eventually have the effect of lightening the mass that keeps us grounded on Earth. The key is the word "eventually"; it's difficult and even, in a sense, cruel to expect us to have that perspective on loss when we're still in the grieving stage.

There's one other attitude that Katrina victims have expressed to the diocesan volunteers: a renewed gratefulness for the life they have. So many of those left behind in the aftermath of the storm have said, in one way or another, that they believe they are honoring the memory of those who died by pushing through the pain and the sorrow. Instead of paralyzing them, their grief has eventually—there's that critical word again—energized them. Despite their losses—or perhaps because of them—they recognize the value of the life they have left.

Walter Anderson, the editor of *Parade* magazine, expressed this perspective well in his book *The Confidence Course: Seven Steps to Self-Fulfillment:* "Although I may not be able to prevent the worst from happening, I am responsible for my attitude toward the inevitable misfortunes that darken life. Bad things do happen; how I respond to them defines my character and the quality of my life. I can choose to sit in perpetual sadness, immobilized by the gravity of my loss, or I can choose to rise

> And God will wipe away every tear from their eyes; there shall be no more death, nor sorrow, nor crying. There shall be no more pain, for the former things have passed away.
>
> —REVELATION 21:4 (NKJV)

from the pain and treasure the most precious gift I have—life itself." Life may be a series of little, and big, give-ups, but it is still a life to be treasured.

REFLECTION

When we suffer a loss, other people can make some incredibly thoughtless, inane, and insensitive remarks, sometimes intentionally but more often out of a cultural discomfort with tragedy, suffering, and loss. We need to remember that the words that count the most during our times of mourning and difficulty are the eternal words of a living God. Meditate on these words of God from Isaiah 43:2, words that assure us that God will be with us through our most trying times:

> When you go through deep waters and great trouble, I will be with you. When you go through rivers of difficulty, you will not drown! When you walk through the fire of oppression, you will not be burned up; the flames will not consume you. (NLT)

PRACTICE

People who have experienced a devastating loss often use the image of a roller-coaster ride to illustrate the frequent emotional lows and occasional highs that follow their loss. They

In this strange life we grow through adversity rather than through success. The greatest lessons we have to learn are those concerned with loss, not gain.

—MARTIN ISRAEL

picture themselves at the highest point on the track right before the loss, which then sends them plummeting to the lowest point. Things start to level out at that point, and then the track begins to rise—and either plateaus or falls again. Using a roller coaster as your image, draw a track that illustrates a time when you suffered a loss. Be honest with yourself; even in a tragic loss, there is often an upside or two. When you can visualize the aftermath of loss—with its highs as well as its lows—you become better prepared to face future losses, knowing that no situation ever remains at its lowest point for very long.

Hope amid Suffering

I have suffered too much in this world not to hope for another.

—**Jean-Jacques Rousseau**

Let's face it: sometimes we bring on our own suffering. Making bad choices, neglecting our health, and worrying needlessly can cause us to suffer, and every one of those causes is our own fault. That doesn't mean we have no hope for a change in our circumstances; it means that we may still have some measure of control over how quickly our circumstances can improve. Our hope is in God, but we can alleviate some of our suffering by using the wisdom and common sense the Spirit gives us.

However, much of the genuine suffering in the world—and in our own lives—results from circumstances far beyond our control. It's also far beyond the scope of this book to grapple with the theological question of why we must suffer; we need to start with the reality of suffering and then look at our response to it.

Author and minister Gerald Mann writes frequently of the lessons suffering has taught him. His wife contracted measles during the early stage of her first pregnancy, and their daughter was born deaf and emotionally disabled. Now an adult with the emotional maturity of a very young child, his daughter has endured a lifetime of medications and rehabilitation and extended separation from her parents. After years of agonizing over and caring for her, Mann discovered this truth about suffering:

> There are two kinds of suffering: self-centered and other-centered. Self-centered suffering is the result of our thinking that the world and God should accommodate themselves to what we want.... Other-centered suffering is our choosing to endure hurt for another.
>
> I decided to get on with my life and try to bring some good out of my suffering. One of the most effective ways I've found to do this is through other-centered suffering. By giving my time and help to my child and to others, I have developed a toughness to persevere which I would not have had otherwise. I have understood life and love in a different way.[8]

Understanding life in a different way is a by-product of hope and goes hand in hand with becoming other-centered in our suffering. Is it possible to experience despair when the focus of our suffering is on others who are also suffering? Of course. But I don't think it's possible to live there for very long and still be of any use to others. Without hope, we would have no basis for believing we could do any good.

My comfort in my suffering is this: Your promise preserves my life.

—PSALM 119:50 (NIV)

The Christian Scriptures in particular support this concept of suffering for the sake of others. Jesus suffered both humiliation and a slow, painful death on the cross for the redemption of all of humanity. What's more, he willingly suffered; Hebrews 12:2 says, "He was willing to die a shameful death on the cross because of the joy he knew would be his afterward" (NLT). That's the ultimate example of other-centered suffering—and hope.

And as it turns out—as it always turns out—God wants us to follow Jesus' example by acquiring a perspective on suffering that goes against the human grain. "My brothers and sisters," writes James at the very beginning of his epistle, "whenever you face trials of any kind, consider it nothing but joy, because you know that the testing of your faith produces endurance" (James 1:2–3, NRSV). Paul saw suffering as an opportunity for a bit of character building: "We also boast in our sufferings, knowing that suffering produces endurance, and endurance produces character, and character produces hope, and hope does not disappoint us, because God's love has been poured into our hearts through the Holy Spirit that has been given to us" (Rom. 5:3–5, NRSV).

But back to the idea of suffering for others. The writer of Hebrews encourages Christians to treat victims of abuse "as if you yourselves were suffering" (Heb. 13:3, NIV), while Paul suggests in the first chapter of Second Corinthians that one of the reasons for our suffering is that when we endure adversity, we are better able to comfort others who are also suffering. And then there's the ultimate example of other-centered human

For it has been granted to you on behalf of Christ not only to believe in him, but also to suffer for him, since you are going through the same struggle you saw I had, and now hear that I still have.

—PHILIPPIANS 1:29–30 (NIV)

37

suffering, again compliments of Paul: "I want to know Christ and the power of his resurrection and the sharing of his sufferings by becoming like him in his death" (Phil. 3:10, NRSV).

Enough of the Bible lesson; where does suffering for others show up in today's world? Think of the stories of heroism that emerged from both the 2004 tsunami in Indonesia and Hurricane Katrina. Ordinary people, if there is such a thing, not only risked their lives for the sake of others during those catastrophes but also endured misery and hardship as they stayed to take care of the victims in the aftermath. They took their focus off their own losses and brought some good out of suffering. I suspect, like Mann, they developed a toughness to persevere that they otherwise would not have had.

Mother Teresa said this of her other-centered work with the poor of Calcutta: "Without our suffering, our work would just be social work, very good and helpful, but it would not be the work of Jesus Christ, not part of the Redemption. All the desolation of the poor people, not only their material poverty, but their spiritual destitution, must be redeemed. And we must share it, for only by being one with them can we redeem them by bringing God into their lives and bringing them to God."[9] Jesus' suffering on the cross comes full circle when we suffer for others with the purpose of bringing God into their lives.

Though we will never fully understand why a loving God allows suffering, we have to admit that the suffering of others can often bring out the best in us. And without the hope that there's a purpose in our sharing in the suffering of others, we'd all be in a sad state indeed.

Out of suffering have emerged the strongest souls; the most massive characters are seared with scars.

—KAHLIL GIBRAN

REFLECTION

What *is* the purpose of suffering? And even if there is a purpose, why does God choose suffering as the means to accomplish that purpose? Have you ever discovered a purpose for the suffering you've endured throughout your life? How has suffering changed you or those around you?

PRACTICE

Helping others puts our own suffering into perspective—even if we think they haven't suffered anywhere near as much as we have! Okay, if we think that, then maybe we're not doing this right. Volunteer, even if it's only a one-time thing, to serve people who are worse off than you are. That could mean the poor or the homeless, but not necessarily. My hospice patients often have homes much nicer than mine, but they're dying, and I'm not; their live-in caregivers are on duty 24/7, and I'm not; those caregivers are often relatives who are pre-grieving, and I'm not. I have it much better, I'd say.

> Although the world is full of suffering, it is full also of the overcoming of it.
> —HELEN KELLER

8 Just How Hopeless Do You Feel?

There are no hopeless situations; there are only people
who have grown hopeless about them.

—Clare Booth Luce

If you want to know how you measure up—or down—in
terms of your feelings of hopelessness, there's a psychological
test you can take that will help you determine whether those
feelings are normal, mild, moderate, or severe. The test is called
the Beck Hopelessness Scale, and among mental health practitioners it serves as a means of predicting a patient's likelihood
of committing suicide. The link between suicide and feelings of
hopelessness, of course, is inarguable.

I've never been under the care of a psychiatrist, so I've never
seen an actual copy of the test. I do know that it is not designed
for self-helpers, which makes sense. After all, if you took the
test on your own and discovered you scored "severely hopeless," it's not very likely that your first thought would be, "Gee,
I need to go out and do something about this!" It's a good idea
to have a professional around when you get the results of a test
like this one.

Even so, recalling those times when depression utterly paralyzed me, I wonder about the effectiveness of such assessments for people like me, even when the test is administered properly. The twenty questions on the Beck test relate to feelings about the future, lack of motivation, and expectations, and all the patient has to do is fill in the appropriate true/false circle. To someone who has never been clinically depressed, it may seem like a fairly easy test to take. But had I attempted to fill out such an evaluation at the time in my life when I felt the most hopeless, I'm certain I would have despaired at its length. I probably would have resorted to filling in the circles so they formed a pleasing pattern on the page, rather than giving serious and honest thought to my answers.

I'm confident tests like that fulfill a needed purpose, and it's not my intention here to call standardized psychological assessments into question. Anything that serves as a barometer for measuring suicidal tendencies is to be welcomed. Some of us, however, still freeze at the sight of a No. 2 pencil. We don't need memories of dreaded achievement tests adding to our despondency.

What some of us may need to do instead is determine how we rate on our own scale of hopelessness—or hopefulness, as the case may be. So here's my suggestion for a personal "do try this at home" variation on the Beck test. Let's say we look at the three broad categories the Beck test focuses on—our feelings about the future, our motivation, and our expectations—and create our own questions. Instead of filling in circles, we could

Hell is hopelessness. It is no accident that above the entrance to Dante's hell is the inscription: "Leave behind all hope, you who enter here."

—FYODOR DOSTOEVSKY

41

spend time reflecting on a question that summarizes each of those areas, something like this:

When I envision my future, what image comes to mind? Maybe you really do see a bottomless abyss, but it's more likely that when you force yourself to visualize your future—even when you're feeling hopeless—you see your life pretty much as it is today. Granted, that can cause you to despair, but you still see *life*. You just need to rearrange the furniture a bit, as it were, and create an image that reflects life as you want it to be.

What would it take—what possibility, what prospect, what promise—to restore the motivation I have lost? Loss of motivation nearly always accompanies loss of hope. After all, what reason do we have to even get out of bed in the morning—or the afternoon, if things are really bad—if we've lost our hope for a better life? Sometimes, all it takes is one opportunity to motivate us to get out of bed and slowly put one foot in front of the other again. We need to always be open to those opportunities so we recognize them when they come.

What are the specific expectations I have for my future? Let's get real here. Let's say you have a reasonably decent life right now, but something has caused you to despair. Do you really expect to be homeless? Bedridden? Alone? In your lowest moments, maybe you do. But if you can give this question some thought at the highest point in your low moments, you'll probably admit that you expect

No one has a right to sit down and feel hopeless. There's too much work to do.

—DOROTHY DAY

your life to get better or at least not get much worse. Deep down, you know that this too shall pass, regardless of what "this" is.

Your answers to those questions, or your own customized versions of those questions, may help you discover that your situation is not as hopeless as you think and that you don't feel all that hopeless after all. Writing out the answers can be amazingly therapeutic; in the course of putting our thoughts down on paper we often reach hopeful conclusions about our lives that we may not otherwise recognize. I can't say the same for filling in circles with a No. 2; that activity has never inspired me to do any serious reflection.

It may be that the time for serious reflection—honest, vulnerable, even painful, reflection—has arrived for you. If you've described your current situation as hopeless, my guess is that the time has in fact arrived and may be overdue. You have everything to gain by searching your life for the hope that lies buried under the all-too-visible despair.

REFLECTION

Ever since the sixteenth century, when St. John of the Cross wrote his now-classic meditation *The Dark Night of the Soul,* Christians and people outside Christianity have used the image expressed in that title to describe periods in their lives when they experienced hopelessness, depression, and the feeling that God had abandoned them. Does this image resonate with

> We are pressed on every side by troubles, but we are not crushed and broken. We are perplexed, but we don't give up and quit. We are hunted down, but God never abandons us. We get knocked down, but we get up again and keep going.
>
> **—2 CORINTHIANS 4:8–9 (NLT)**

43

you? If not, what image would describe the lowest points in your life?[10]

PRACTICE

Look back over the three main questions in this chapter. If you did not answer them earlier, take the time to answer them now. For each question, also write down your best guess as to how your answer would be different if you felt more hopeful about your life. Record your answers somewhere—on paper, in your computer, anywhere more permanent than in your memory alone. Revisit them in a month. See how your answers have changed, if at all. Small, incremental steps toward a more hopeful way of living do add up. Even the small act of writing down the answers to those three questions can have a greater impact than you think.

The important thing is not that we can live on hope alone, but that life is not worth living without it.

—HARVEY MILK

Overcoming Hopelessness

9

When you say a situation or a person is hopeless, you are slamming the door in the face of God.

—Charles L. Allen

Let's say you've taken the Beck test described in the previous reflection and you've discovered that your perspective on life is indeed one of genuine hopelessness. Let's also say that you have the good sense to get professional help from both a mental health practitioner and a spiritual adviser. What else can you do to help overcome the pervasive sense of hopelessness that dominates your thinking?

For one thing, you can turn to Frances Moore Lappé—that's right, the author of *Diet for a Small Planet*—for some pretty sound advice. In a highly recommended online course, "Solutions to Violence,"[11] Lappé correctly connects hopelessness with powerlessness. Though she is discussing these concepts in relation to social justice issues, her identification of the problem and the solutions she offers also work on a personal level. People who feel powerless to stop the spread of AIDS in Africa begin to consider the situation hopeless; likewise, the less power we feel that we have over our personal lives, the more hopeless we are bound to feel.

To regain both our empowerment and our hopefulness, Lappé writes, we need to (1) live lives consistent with our beliefs; (2) take responsibility for our actions; (3) be open to change; and (4) be willing to take risks. If we look at these four steps—again, intended to be used in a social justice context—within the framework of our spirituality, it's evident that they can contribute to helping us overcome our hopelessness.

We need to live lives consistent with our beliefs. Many people, I'm guessing, will find that their lack of hope stems from a life that contradicts their basic belief system. If we say we believe God loves us and is actively involved in our lives, and yet we fail to turn to God when we become discouraged, it's no wonder that despair and hopelessness begin to plague our lives.

We need to take responsibility for our actions. We sometimes need to take responsibility for actions that caused us to despair in the first place, such as financial recklessness. But we always need to take responsibility for what we do after the fact, even when our actions in no way contributed to the cause. Facing a predicament head on is empowering, even when the situation appears to be truly hopeless—just ask a terminally ill cancer patient who has decided that he is going to live life to the fullest for as long as possible. The outcome may be the same, but the journey

Isn't it the moment of most profound doubt that gives birth to new certainties? Perhaps hopelessness is the very soil that nourishes human hope; perhaps one could never find sense in life without first experiencing its absurdity.

—VACLAV HAVEL

changes dramatically when we own up to the circumstances we find ourselves in.

We must be open to change. Hopelessness resists change because hopelessness resists action. But change is necessary if we are to live lives consistent with our beliefs, because acquiring that consistency involves spiritual transformation. So, if we get past step one, we're well on our way toward accomplishing step three. See how easy this is getting?

We must be willing to take risks. Maybe I spoke too soon. Maybe these steps are tough going for those who like to play it safe. But as Lappé writes, "There is no change without risk. To change, we must push ourselves to do what we thought we were incapable of doing." See? There's a good chance you've been taking risks without even knowing it. But what kinds of risks are related to overcoming hopelessness? The risk that the people in your life will think you are a fool for placing your hope in God. The risk that you won't have what it takes to live a life consistent with your beliefs, that you will fail spiritually. The risk that by taking responsibility for your actions, more will be expected of you than you can deliver. The risk that you'll feel no more hopeful tomorrow than you do today.

The risk that you'll be proven wrong.

That last risk is so big that it warrants its own space on the page. Being proven wrong is no fun. Most of us like to be right,

Our soul waits for the Lord; He is our help and our shield. For our heart shall rejoice in Him, because we have trusted in His holy name. Let Your mercy, O Lord, be upon us, just as we hope in You.

—PSALM 33:20–22 (NKJV)

and we like to be right all the time. It's especially galling when we express an optimistic attitude, and the world crumbles beneath our feet. The ever-wise Ms. Lappé offers this suggestion: "We must choose friends and colleagues who will push us to do what we thought we could not do. But we must select friends who will 'catch' us, too, when we push ourselves too far and need to be supported." There's nothing like a supportive friend to help us take risks, as well as pick us up when our efforts fail. If your supportive friend shares your spiritual beliefs all the better; you won't run the *added* risk of having to justify the hope that lies within you. Enough is enough when it comes to risk taking.

Lappé's four steps appear to be deceptively simple. Common sense often appears to be simple, too, but it can solve a whole range of problems. Lappé's advice, taken in tandem with that ever-important professional help, is worth heeding, whether we're hopeless or not.

It is only when everything is hopeless that hope begins to be a strength.

—G. K. CHESTERTON

REFLECTION

Sometimes our hopelessness reflects the futility we feel when we've worked hard for someone or something, but we see no results, no respect for us or our efforts, and no reward, even if the only reward we expect is personal satisfaction. The writer of Hebrews understood the hopelessness experienced by the early followers of Jesus as they sought to serve both God and people. This is what he wrote to encourage them:

God is fair; he will not forget the work you did and the love you showed for him by helping his people. And he will remember that you are still helping them. We want each of you to go on with the same hard work all your lives so you will surely get what you hope for. We do not want you to become lazy. Be like those who through faith and patience will receive what God has promised. (Hebrews 6:10–12, (NCV)

Reflect on that passage as if it had been written specifically for you. Break the passage down into smaller segments—such as "God is fair" or "you will surely get what you hope for" or "what God has promised"—and zero in on those portions and determine specifically what they mean to you and whether or not you believe them. Then pray one of the most honest pleas in the Bible, the desperate cry of a father for his son, found in Mark 9:24: "I believe; help my unbelief!"

PRACTICE

Imagine that you are God. Seriously. Don't try to change the universe or anything, but do try to imagine God's perspective on a situation in your life that seems hopeless to you. As an example, let's take something basic, such as an estrangement from a friend who once meant the world to you. You've had a major falling out; let's say you unintentionally offended her,

Life without faith in something is too narrow a space to live.
—GEORGE LANCASTER SPALDING

49

and although you've tried to apologize and express the value you place on your relationship, she will not respond to your emails, answer the phone when you call, or open the door when you try to visit.

Begin by writing down a brief list of words and phrases that describe the way you see or feel about the situation—sorry, annoyed that she took it the wrong way, sad that she seems to value your friendship less than you do, and so forth. Now do the same for your friend, but here your list will only reflect your *assumptions* about how she feels—offended, angry, betrayed, maybe even ashamed that she has let the rift last so long. Finally, imagine how God—or if that makes you uncomfortable, someone objective and omniscient who can see into the hearts of man and woman, someone just like … um, God—perceives the situation. Write down what you think God sees in your heart and in your friend's heart.

The simple act of looking at the situation from different perspectives can help you not only to better understand the estrangement but also to explore other ways of mending it, if you still feel that the relationship can be restored. Ask God for creative ways to approach your friend. And don't forget the single most important ingredient in healing any relationship—chocolate. Hold it—I mean forgiveness. Forgive your friend for ignoring you. Forgive yourself for offending her. Keep on forgiving until you've covered all those bases that need to be touched by forgiveness.

Real and Imagined Threats

In the face of uncertainty, there is nothing wrong with hope.
—Dr. Bernie Siegel

In an insightful column expressing outrage at Americans' lack of outrage over the news that the government has been tracking our phone calls, *Washington Post* writer Eugene Robinson offered up this wonderful visual analysis of what ails us as a nation:

> If a psychiatrist were to put the nation on the couch, the shrink's notes would read something like this: "Patient feels vulnerable to attack; cannot remember having experienced similar feeling before. Patient accustomed to being in control; now feels buffeted by outside forces beyond grasp. Patient believes livelihood and prosperity being usurped by others (repeatedly mentions China). Patient seeks scapegoats for personal failings (immigrants, Muslims, civil libertarians). Patient is by far most powerful nation in world, yet feels powerless. Patient is full of unfocused anger."[12]

Every area of trouble gives out a ray of hope, and the one unchangeable certainty is that nothing is certain or unchangeable.

—JOHN F. KENNEDY

We do live in a time of uncertainty, don't we? On September 10, 2001, we were the most powerful nation in the world, and we knew it. A day later, we faced the reality that we could be taken down. Despite the rhetoric from politicians and leaders who have trumpeted America's greatness ever since 9/11, many of us are not so sure anymore about our greatness. If we're so great, how could one terrorist group cause so much devastation to our country and so much damage to our collective psyche? If we're so great, how come so many manufacturers have fled to other countries, and how come many that remain can't produce a quality product? If we're so great, why can't we get the rest of the world to like us?

As we lie on the couch waiting for the psychiatrist, who we're convinced is busy with far more important patients, we wonder: "Am I paranoid, or are these threats, these perceptions, these fears valid?" After more intolerable waiting, we answer our own question: "Probably both." And then we ask another question: "So who needs a shrink?" We already have the answer.

We're back to square one, but at least we've been able to admit that the very real threats to our safety and security have created a cultural paranoia. The question now is: "What are we going to do about it?"

I like this thought from mind-body expert and best-selling author Dr. Bernie Siegel: "In the face of uncertainty, there's nothing wrong with hope." When it comes to the real threats, the best we can do is remain vigilant and support the government's efforts—the reasonable ones, that is—to keep us safe. (Better security at airports, train and bus stations, and shipping ports is a reasonable effort, even if it inconveniences me. Probing into my phone records to discover that I called my gynecologist on June 8 at 2:26 p.m. is not reasonable.)

When it comes to our paranoia, there's plenty we can do. Here are some things I've learned about nonclinical, garden-variety paranoia (which several mental-health experts have dubbed "paranoia lite")—not that I've ever had firsthand experience with it or anything:

Paranoid people ignore color wheels. Everything's black or white—that's it. Learning to see the gray, and all those other colors, helps immensely in avoiding or overcoming paranoia. One of the best moves I've ever made was toward a "gray" perspective with regard to political parties. It keeps my anger in check, and it helps me to make wiser choices in the voting booth. Graying our perspectives also enables us to maintain a fair and reasonable attitude toward ethnic groups, regional factions, political parties, and religious persuasions.

Paranoid people make lousy Buddhists. That's because they can't get the hang of living in the moment. Learning from the past and preparing for the future are critical skills to have, but trying to live in either dimension will only make you crazy. Enjoy this moment—*this* one, right now. And then enjoy the next moment when it comes. It's awfully hard to remain fearful and threatened for very long when you live in the moment.

Ah, what a dusty answer gets this soul when hot for certainties, in this, our life!

—George Meredith

53

Paranoid people make great egomaniacs. After all, the world is out to get them, so why shouldn't they be obsessed with their very own selves? In all the volunteer work I've done, I can honestly say that I've never met a committed volunteer with a heart to serve others who gave any hint of being fearful or paranoid. When we begin to live outside our own heads and start to live in service to others, it's amazing how quickly our perspective on life changes for the better.

Paranoid people are the death of the party. They have no sense of humor. None. Everything is deadly serious. By lightening up and allowing ourselves a little amusement— even about deadly serious matters—we become increasingly aware of just how comical our rigid, intense perspective is. There's nothing like Comedy Central's *The Daily Show* or *The Colbert Report* to help us put world events in perspective.

Paranoid people live in tight spaces. Small world, narrow focus, limited viewpoint. What kind of life is that? Broadening our perspective on life makes room for the best antidote of all to paranoia—hope.

I say we abolish paranoia lite altogether. Let's train our minds to stop thinking and worrying about things that may not ever happen. See the gray, live in the moment, serve others, lighten up, expand our world. Not a bad prescription for living with uncertainty.

REFLECTION

Several years ago a scholarly book about the current challenges facing the Jesuit order was released. The content of the book is not as relevant here as is its title: *Passionate Uncertainty*. Think about that phrase. What are you passionate about despite the uncertainty of the situation? What is it that fuels your enthusiasm despite the ambiguity? Some, if not many, people remain passionate about their faith even though they are unsure why they believe what they believe. Does that kind of uncertainty resonate with you?

PRACTICE

In the days following 9/11, many of us developed coping strategies, even though at the time we were oblivious to the fact that that's what we were doing. In the intervening years, I've come to appreciate some of the measures I took to keep things in perspective, which was especially critical in 2001 when my daughters were both teenagers. These are just a few practical guidelines for living with uncertainty:

- Learn all you can about the situation without becoming morbidly obsessive. Like many people, I watched television nonstop right after the attacks (I happened to be watching a morning news show when they occurred, so I

Hope and hopelessness persist despite the facts.

—MASON COOLEY

May those who fear you rejoice when they see me, for I have put my hope in your word.

—**Psalm 119:74 (NIV)**

was inundated with those horrific images from the moment they first aired). But within a few days I turned the television off, took a break from the horror of it all, and began reading up on terrorism and Islam from reliable sources. If your uncertainty is related to a health issue or finances or any other area of your life, learn all you can about the problem and the solutions—again, from reliable sources. Sometimes what we learn can be frightening, but that knowledge can also empower us if we allow it to.

• Return to your normal routine as soon as possible. "As soon as possible" is a relative concept, of course. In the aftermath of a minor fire in our home, we were displaced for almost two months—two months filled with uncertainty about things such as what our insurance would and wouldn't cover, which is never as clear-cut as it should be; what needed to be done to the house, and when and how it would get done; how much danger we had been exposed to by inhaling toxins right after the fire. Six months later, we're still not back to normal. We've returned to our usual routines, even though that delays restoring our house to its former condition.

- Talk things out, but avoid unhealthy dis-
  agreements and attitudes. No matter how
  legitimate your anxiety over the war in Iraq
  may be, digging your heels in and engaging
  in pointless debates with those who disagree
  with you will only increase your anxiety level.
  Be patient and gracious with those who try to
  fix you and your situation; some people don't
  understand that when you're expressing your
  feelings, all you want is a listening ear, not a
  prescription. If you tell a friend that you've
  just been diagnosed with diabetes, and he
  launches into a detailed description of the
  perfect diet and treatment plan that he just
  knows will work for you, take a deep breath,
  remind yourself that he means well, take
  another deep breath, and ask God for a triple
  dose of patience.

- I know you don't want to hear this, because I
  never like to hear it either, but it really is
  important to eat right and stay active in times
  of high anxiety. Living and working from a
  makeshift office in a hotel room with nothing
  more than a refrigerator and microwave
  wrought havoc on my dietary health, but I
  ran around handling so many fire-related
  chores that I managed to compensate for the
  intake of restaurant and fast food (which

made me gag after a while). The "running around" was fairly stressful and hardly qualifies as exercise, but you take what you can get sometimes. Anyway, the right food and the right level of activity really do help decrease our anxiety.

Hope Dies Last

La esperanza muere al último.

Hope dies last.

—Mexican Proverb

Pulitzer Prize–winning author Studs Terkel frequently quotes a farm worker who later became a union organizer and worked with activist Cesar Chavez to fight for the rights of farm and migrant workers in California and elsewhere. "We have a saying," Jessie De La Cruz once told Terkel. "*La esperanza muere al último.* Hope dies last."

It was in 1964 that Jessie first got involved in the movement that would eventually result in the creation of the United Farm Workers union. Chavez and his followers helped improve the deplorable and largely unregulated working and living conditions of hundreds of thousands of immigrant workers.

Forty-two years later—keep that number in your head—a team of young journalism students did a series of radio specials for the University of North Carolina. One student, Krista Keck, reported on the work of Letitia Zavala, whose family came to the United States illegally. Letitia is a rarity; she began working in the fields at the age of eight, but went on to receive

59

As long as there is one upright man, as long as there is one compassionate woman, the contagion may spread and the scene is not desolate. Hope is the thing left to us in a bad time.

—E. B. WHITE

a college scholarship and earn a degree in business administration; she's now an organizing director for the AFL-CIO's Farm Labor Organizing Committee, and she spends her days back in the fields, working to help migrant farm workers. Krista accompanied her one day as she made her rounds to various farms in eastern North Carolina and reported on the migrant workers'—you guessed it—deplorable working and living conditions. Forty-two years later activists were still at it, fighting for basic human needs.

Toward the end of their day together, Letitia became reflective. "In Spanish there's a saying that says *la esperanza muere al ultimo* … hope dies last … and yeah, that's the way many of us function," she told Krista. "We just keep praying and hoping that one day there is going to be a time that every worker is respected and every worker is treated the way they should be treated."

It's haunting to hear her echo the very words Jessie De La Cruz used so many decades earlier to describe the one thing the farm owners could not kill—their hope. Like Jessie, Letitia worked the fields, left the fields, and could have settled into a nice office job away from the fields. Instead, both women returned to the fields because the hope they had for the future well-being of migrant workers just would not die. That, despite a host of obstacles that should have discouraged them at every turn.

Governmental wage and labor agencies fail to thoroughly investigate dishonest employers. Building inspectors turn a blind eye to housing-code violations. Social workers who actually try to do some good don't last very long, sometimes because of the hazardous conditions they face. The health and safety of farm and migrant workers isn't exactly a high priority among agencies that regulate workplace conditions, which means social workers and migrant advocates like Letitia are also subjected to workplace hazards when they visit the farms.

A social worker I once knew always wore long-sleeved shirts, even on the hottest days here in central Florida. At a Bible study one night at our church, she looked so uncomfortable that someone suggested she roll up her sleeves to cool off a bit. "This is why I don't do that," she said, as she pulled one sleeve up just far enough for us to see an ugly rash caused by chemicals that the area's fern growers spray on the plants. Like the farm workers she visited, she was living with the consequences of working in a hazardous environment, but she refused to give up. Hope was the fuel that kept her praying week after week for the safety and protection of the workers she served.

When we feel we've exhausted every last resource in our efforts to bring about change—whether it's in the living conditions of migrant workers or in the crumbling condition of a special relationship in our life—hope becomes the fuel that keeps us going and keeps us believing that a better day will come, maybe even tomorrow. "Without hope," Studs Terkel said once in an interview about Jessie De La Cruz, "you become just a cynic, and that's a dime a dozen." One thing we don't need is more cynics, and we certainly don't need anything that might fuel our own tendency toward cynicism. No, we need a ready reserve of the kind of hope that never dies. Or at the very least, the kind that dies last.

> What oxygen is to the lungs, such is hope to the meaning of life.
> —EMIL BRUNNER

REFLECTION

One of the hardest realities we face when we're working to bring about needed change is the fact that we may never see the fruit of our labor. And yet we keep at it, because we can't do otherwise. We need to always remember that throughout history the most significant reforms were never enacted quickly. The groundwork for reform was laid years, and even centuries, before any real change took place. Look at this thought from social theorist Erich Fromm, author of the highly recommended *The Art of Loving,* and many other great books:

> To hope means to be ready at every moment for
> that which is not yet born, and yet not become des-
> perate if there is no birth in our lifetime.

You're probably more than ready for that which is not yet born, but have you become desperate to witness its birth? Desperation can rob you of hope. How can you maintain your readiness without losing your hope?

PRACTICE

Make it a point to talk to someone who is so committed to a cause that they keep on going despite every hurdle that pops up in front of them. The "cause" doesn't have to be political or social; healthcare professionals who work with the terminally

If one truly has lost hope, one would not be around to say so.

—ERIC BENTLEY

62

ill, paralytics, or the mentally ill also qualify, as do people whose work can be particularly frustrating at times—like clergy or leaders in any capacity (all you have to do is become the leader of a small group in your faith community to marvel at those who willingly and repeatedly take on leadership roles!). Find out what it is that keeps these committed individuals going, how they perceive obstacles and frustrations, and how they've learned to handle them. The wisdom of people who have been in the trenches can be of enormous help when we become discouraged at not seeing any progress in our own projects.

Of all the forces that make for a better world, none is so indispensable, none so powerful, as hope. Without hope men are only half alive. With hope they dream and think and work.

—CHARLES SAWYER

12
Holding On to Hope

True hope dwells on the possible, even when life seems
to be a plot written by someone who wants to see how
much adversity we can overcome. True hope responds
to the real world, to real life; it is an active effort.

—**Walter Anderson**

There's one morning in 1983 that I will never forget, even
though nothing earth-shattering took place. It was the first
time our daughter Elizabeth slept through the night. She was
only two weeks old, and when I awoke at 7 a.m. and realized
my newborn had not summoned me for a feeding in more than
eight hours, my whole being filled with dread. I was so terror-
stricken that I walked the twenty or so feet to her room more
slowly than usual. I needed the extra time to pull myself
together and brace for the worst. To this day, I consider that to
be the longest walk I've taken in my entire life.

As new parents, we try not to think of all the things that
could go wrong. But in the back of our minds, disorders like
sudden infant death syndrome loom large. I had never heard of
an infant so young sleeping so long without a feeding. When I
approached her crib and saw that she was sleeping soundly, I

collapsed in a rocking chair and just let the tears stream down my face until she woke up a few minutes later.

I cannot imagine the grief that accompanies the death of a child. It's too much for me to comprehend. I look at women who have miscarried or had a stillbirth or lost a child they had loved, nurtured, and cherished for days or years, and I ache for them, even years after their loss. But of all the mothers I've known who have suffered loss, there's one whose name always brings tears to my eyes. Her name is Nancy Guthrie, and you may know her story.

In 1998, Nancy gave birth to a beautiful girl that she and her husband, David, had decided to name Hope. Little did they know how much hope they would need to make it through each day in the coming months and years. Within two days of Hope's birth, a geneticist delivered the news to the Guthries that their precious daughter likely suffered from a rare disorder called Zellweger syndrome. The prognosis was not good; babies born with the disorder usually died within six months.

Throughout their marriage and even before, the Guthries had always maintained a strong faith in God; in fact, the two met when they both worked for Word, a Christian publishing house. Their first child, Matt, had been born perfectly healthy, and they had no reason to suspect that the situation would be any different with their second child. The news of Hope's condition blindsided them—as did the news that the odds of both parents carrying the recessive gene *and* having a baby born with Zellweger syndrome were minuscule. Gerald Raymond of the Kennedy Krieger Institute at Johns Hopkins University, the

We must embrace pain and burn it as fuel for our journey.
—KENJI MIYAZAWA

65

only place where the testing is done, told the Guthries that there are only about twenty children diagnosed with Zellweger syndrome in the United States each year. The Guthries were a rarity among rarities. They struggled to make sense of the card they had been dealt.

Hope lived 199 days. Saddened beyond measure, the Guthries decided that it was not wise to risk having another child with the same disorder, so David had a vasectomy. The odds that Nancy would become pregnant again were one in two thousand. Eighteen months later, though, Nancy was in fact pregnant—and the child, a boy, would also be born with Zellweger syndrome. Abortion was an option, but not one that Nancy and David considered; they had learned from their experience with Hope that a life does not have to be long or of a certain quality to be valuable or cherished. Gabriel was born on July 16, 2001, the same date of the issue of *Time* magazine that carried an article about the Guthries and their journey of faith to that point. Gabe died less than six months later.

Anyone even marginally familiar with the Bible should be thinking of Job right about now. Job was considered the greatest man of his time, but he lost everything in the twinkling of an eye—his family, his home, his possessions—everything. And with God's blessing, no less; as the story goes, it was God who gave Satan permission to meddle in Job's life. With good reason, Job is considered the prime biblical example of human suffering.

Ironically, Nancy had completed a study of the book of Job right before Hope's birth. Job's story gradually became so intri-

Be of good courage, and He shall strengthen your heart, all you who hope in the Lord.

—PSALM 31:24 (NKJV)

cately woven into her own that she turned their merged stories into the book *Holding On to Hope: A Pathway through Suffering to the Heart of God.* Its pages contain some of the most honest and vulnerable and poignant thoughts on suffering, and God's hand in suffering, that I have ever read.

I've connected with Nancy once or twice a year over the past decade at a Christian publishing trade show where, as the director of media relations for the sponsoring organization, she puts up with journalists like me. Because I'm always well out of any and every loop, I had heard about Hope's birth but not about the diagnosis. So the next time I saw Nancy, I cheerily congratulated her. Nancy delivered the devastating news about Hope's death with nothing short of an amazing grace, even though I'm sure my breezy remark must have hit her like a punch in the gut. When I heard about Gabriel several years later, it was too much to take; now, whenever Nancy's name crosses my mind or appears in my inbox, my eyes fill up with tears. But I'm just a bystander, and a very distant one at that.

"Sometimes what God has allowed into our lives is so bitter that we're hurt and angry and don't even want to talk to him about it," Guthrie writes in *Holding On to Hope.* "But where does that leave us? On our own. No resources, no truth to dispel the despair, no hope.

"The truth is, there is no comfort to be found away from God; at least, there is no lasting, deep, satisfying comfort. Revenge, ritual, retreat—they don't bring any lasting relief from the pain. Only the truth of God's Word, the tenderness of his welcome, the touch of his healing presence bring the kind of comfort we crave. Only his promises of purpose in this life and perfection in the life to come offer us any kind of real hope to hold on to."

Nancy, David, and Matt Guthrie have walked a profoundly sad path. But instead of leading them away from God, the path led them to a deeper devotion to God. Along the way, they discovered an understanding of the nature of hope—hope that has been tested to an unimaginable degree—that most of us will never comprehend.

REFLECTION

In a chapter titled "Mystery," Nancy Guthrie writes:

> Our task is not to decipher exactly how all of life's pieces fit and what they all mean but to remain faithful and obedient to God, who knows all mysteries. That is the kind of faith that is pleasing to God—a faith that is determined to trust him when he has not answered all the questions, when we have not heard the voice from the whirlwind.

That last phrase is taken from Job 38 (and also appears in Job 40, in a similar context). If you have never read Job or have not read it in a while, it's well worth reading and reflecting on. If nothing else, find the time to read all of chapter 38, which is priceless in its wisdom and literary quality. Here are the first few verses:

Then the Lord answered Job from the whirlwind: "Who is this that questions my wisdom with such ignorant words? Brace yourself, because I have some questions for you, and you must answer them. Where were you when I laid the foundations of the earth? Tell me, if you know so much. Do you know how its dimensions were determined and who did the surveying? What supports its foundations, and who laid its cornerstone as the morning stars sang together and all the angels shouted for joy? Who defined the boundaries of the sea as it burst from the womb, and as I clothed it with clouds and thick darkness? For I locked it behind barred gates, limiting its shores. I said, 'Thus far and no farther will you come. Here your proud waves must stop!'" (Job 38:1–11, NLT)

> There are no statistics when it comes to tragedy. There are just stories.
>
> —GREGORY FLOYD

As you read, consider these questions: Are you comfortable with the idea of religious mystery—that there are some biblical concepts we will never comprehend, some answers we will never get from God, some areas of spiritual life in which our knowledge will always remain incomplete? Are you willing to trust God completely, in light of those mysteries?

PRACTICE

Going public with their story of grief meant reliving their sorrow over and over again for Nancy and David—first, in the interview with *Time* magazine and the publicity that resulted. Publication of *Holding On to Hope* and a subsequent book, *The One Year Book of Hope,* brought more media attention and requests for the Guthries to share their story at churches and other locations.

We all have a significant story to tell, because every life is significant. We may not have endured hardship or suffered an enormous loss; we may not have made a name for ourselves through our astonishing success; we may not have provided an endless supply of inspiration or wisdom or even amusement for our countless followers. But we still have a story to tell, a story of surpassing greatness because of the surpassing greatness of God. Tell the story of what God has done in your life, with regard to one specific incident or to the whole package. Share it with someone—or many someones. Reread it yourself, and don't be surprised if you start to feel more grateful than ever for the life you live and the God you love.

The Heart of Healing

13

> Hope helps us overcome hurdles that we otherwise could not scale, and it moves us forward to a place where healing can occur.... I see hope as the very heart of healing.
> —**Jerome Groopman**

Because I find the connection between our emotions and our physical well-being intriguing, I gravitate on occasion toward the body-mind-health sections of bookstores and the corresponding shelves in libraries. Part of what I find so fascinating is the abundance of hooey—a technical term for "bunk"—in the books I find there. I mean, really. I'm not exactly the biggest fan of the American Medical Association or the processed food industry, and I believe in alternative medical care and keeping foods as close to their original state as possible, but as I said— really, now. Scanning the titles in the health and wellness section of any major bookstore makes for an endlessly amusing outing.

Imagine my joy when I realized that a book whose title I found especially intriguing—*The Anatomy of Hope*—was written by someone who knows what he's talking about and never once advocates following a blood-type diet. That someone is

Dr. Jerome Groopman, a Harvard Medical School professor, oncologist, and hematologist who has done significant work with AIDS patients. His inspirations for writing the book were the many patients whose positive responses to therapies and treatments appeared to correspond directly to the hope they expressed in words and exhibited in their lives.

As a physician whose work is steeped in research in a number of specialties, Groopman found the correlation between hope and healing so compelling that he began to study the connection on a clinical level. In addition to case studies of patients suffering from a wide range of illnesses and disorders, Groopman includes an account of his own debilitating back pain and the role his feelings of hopelessness played in worsening the situation.

"Hope sets off a chain reaction," he asserts. "Hope tempers pain, and as we sense less pain, that feeling of hope expands, which further reduces pain."[13] Wow—that's a fairly bold statement and one I hope and pray is true. As one of the millions of Americans who suffer chronic pain of one type or another, I now feel more hopeful than ever that I may someday be pain-free, or at least less pain-full. If he's right, I'm doubling up on my daily hope intake, even though I don't have any idea how to do that. I'll figure it out somehow.

Just as exercise does, belief and expectation—which Groopman identifies as the key elements of hope—release endorphins that block pain. Hope also impacts the respiratory and circulation systems and motor function—and because all our bodily systems and functions are interrelated, hope has a

> The capacity for hope is the most significant fact of life. It provides human beings with a sense of destination and the energy to get started.
>
> —NORMAN COUSINS

domino effect, improving each system like a link in a chain. This, he writes, "changes us profoundly in spirit and in body."[14]

Still, Groopman does not suggest that hope can cure an incurable disease or that every optimistic patient gets better or lives longer. Regardless of the ultimate outcome of their particular medical problem, he writes, those who have hope "live better." One patient who accepted the fact that he had little chance of survival refused to yield to disease, finding hope in the battle itself. Though he knew he would die, he reveled over the sheer fact that he had the strength to continue the fight. His victory came through waging the battle, not winning the war.

That's an example of what Groopman identifies as true hope—the ability to accept reality and find the best way around the obstacles within that reality. Patients with false hope, he writes, fail to accept reality and thus run the risk of making poor choices and flawed decisions. Finally, patients who demonstrate no evidence of hope are those who feel they have lost control of their own lives and are now at the mercy of forces outside of themselves. Those are the patients least likely to respond well to treatment.

Hopelessness blinds us to the opportunities and possibilities in many areas of our lives, including our health and well-being. We have no hope of losing weight, so we can't see any benefit in eating right. We have no hope of running a marathon, so we can't see the point of taking a walk every day. We have no hope of bench-pressing five hundred pounds, so we can't see any reason to lift a five-pound hand weight.

There is no medicine like hope, no incentive so great, no tonic so powerful as expectation of something tomorrow.

—ORISON SWETT MARDEN

Now that I've reached "a certain age," I find I'm becoming more focused on the quality of the rest of my life than the length of the rest of my life. I'll forgo the supergreens and superfoods and all other miracle products in favor of a healthy dose of hope. It may not help me live longer, but I'm convinced Groopman is right when he says it will help me live better. See if it isn't the same for you.

REFLECTION

Read the following passage from the Gospel of John:

> Near the Sheep Gate in Jerusalem there was a pool, in Hebrew called Bethesda, with five alcoves. Hundreds of sick people—blind, crippled, paralyzed—were in these alcoves. One man had been an invalid there for thirty-eight years. When Jesus saw him stretched out by the pool and knew how long he had been there, he said, "Do you want to get well?" The sick man said, "Sir, when the water is stirred, I don't have anybody to put me in the pool. By the time I get there, somebody else is already in." Jesus said, "Get up, take your bedroll, start walking." The man was healed on the spot. He picked up his bedroll and walked off. (John 5:2–9, *The Message*)

Now read it again, this time placing yourself in the role of the man who had been an invalid for thirty-eight years, sub-

Hope is the physician of each misery.

—IRISH PROVERB

stituting your own medical condition for his. Imagine your-self waiting on the sidelines for years, knowing that your healing was within reach but that you were incapable of obtaining it. The one person you know who could help you approaches and asks what seems to be a patently absurd question: "Do you want to get well?" Let your imagination take it from there. See what God wants to show you through this exercise.

PRACTICE

Ever since *Saturday Review* editor Norman Cousins cited Marx Brothers movies as a factor in his miraculous recovery from a debilitating illness, the medical community has studied the relationship between laughter and healing. Cousins called laughter "internal jogging," with the added benefit that you didn't have to go outside to exercise. Laughter, he observed, "moves your internal organs around. It enhances respiration. It is an igniter of great expectations." Numerous medical studies agree and even go further; laughter helps muscles relax, relieves pain, strengthens the immune system, reduces stress, lowers blood pressure, improves cardiac conditioning, and benefits respiration.

This next suggestion may not be for everyone, though laughter-therapy advocates suggest it is. They insist it gets easier the more you try it. I remain unconvinced, but several people I have a great deal of respect for claim that it has changed their lives by improving their physical and mental health. Here goes:

It takes courage to live—courage and strength and hope and humor. And courage and strength and hope and humor have to be bought and paid for with pain and work and prayers and tears.
—JEROME P. FLEISCHMAN

Every morning when you get out of bed, after a nice, slow stretch, spend five minutes just laughing. If you need a prompt, start out with "ha-ha-ha, ho-ho-ho" or something equally absurd, and you'll eventually start laughing at how ridiculous you sound (and maybe at how ridiculous the exercise is, but that could just be me). Do the same thing at night right before you go to bed.

I will say this: I've done this in a group setting, and I totally cracked up. It really was therapeutic. I've tried to recreate the magic privately, but I probably gave up too soon. I'll try it again someday. Or maybe I'll just watch reruns of *Monk* to regain my health and sanity.

The Unreturned Prodigal

14

Every parent is at some time the father of the unreturned
prodigal, with nothing to do but keep his house open to
hope.

—John Ciardi

People of faith who are also parents of prodigals share an
unspoken bond, a connection deep within that speaks of both
hope and despair—or, more likely, that alternates between the
two with the scales too often tipped by the crushing weight of
despair. Their adult children have chosen lives so markedly
opposed to everything their parents wanted for them that it's
tough for those parents to keep on believing, keep on praying,
keep on hoping.

While children are young and still living at home, it's much
easier to have hope for them, isn't it? In all but the most
extreme cases, a rebellious, defiant child occasionally exhibits
some kind of behavior that mirrors the way they were at a more
innocent time in their lives. It may be something as simple as a
witty remark or a fleeting but joyful facial expression, but it's
enough to keep hoping that things could return to the way they
once were. It's not as easy to hold on to that hope, though, after
those defiant children leave home—especially when you

know they've traded in a life of promise for a life of diminished possibilities.

And then there's the pesky verse in Proverbs that parents want to believe but would rather ignore: "Teach your children to choose the right path, and when they are older, they will remain upon it" (Prov. 22:6, NLT). Some say it's a principle; if you train your children in the right way, then generally they will choose the right path when they grow up. Others, though, see it as a promise, a guarantee that if you do parenthood right, your children will do adulthood right. For parents of prodigals, neither interpretation offers much comfort. They're left with two choices: they were lousy parents, or God does not make good on either promises or principles.

At one time in particular, prodigals presented a very real problem for their parents in a charismatic church I belonged to. The church was relatively new, maybe ten years old, and many of its members had either returned to the God they had once known or had come to faith for the first time through the ministry of the church. Their lives had been dramatically transformed, and they believed that their adult children's lives could be similarly changed. But here they were, nearly a decade later, still despairing over the way their children were living.

Who could blame them? Broken marriages, alcoholism, drug abuse, prostitution—all of these factors and more characterized the lives of some of the adult children represented in that church. To add to the fears of their parents, an even greater threat had recently reared its ugly, destructive head: AIDS. The son of one couple had already been diagnosed; many other par-

Do not, therefore, abandon that confidence of yours; it brings a great reward. For you need endurance, so that when you have done the will of God, you may receive what was promised.

—Hebrews 10:35–36 (NRSV)

ents held their breath, praying that their sons would not be next. They would soon learn that their daughters needed those same prayers.

Amid this atmosphere of hopelessness, our pastor recognized the need for a series of sermons on hope. One Sunday, he stopped in the middle of his sermon and looked out over the congregation; I believed then and still believe that he had not planned this little interruption. I suspect he looked out at all those fearful faces and knew his words were inadequate for the situation. What he needed was a demonstration of the power of hope—hope for all those prodigals who were risking so much for so little.

"Those of you who have adult children that you're praying for, children who have left the faith or never embraced the faith and are now living apart from God, I want you to stand," he said, as his eyes scanned the room. One by one they stood, some a bit more slowly than others—a few men and a great many women whose faces betrayed their sorrow and grief and utter desolation. Some were hunched over, their bodies weighed down by the burdens they were carrying. Others stood stiffly, but the tears streaming down their cheeks gave them away.

The rest of us sat and watched and waited as the pastor tried to offer a few words of consolation and encouragement to the parents, something along the lines of "Never give up hope." His words seemed to do little good.

But what he said next—well, that made all the difference. He continued, "Now, those of you who were once wayward children, who in your adult years had strayed far from God but

> We do not cease to be children because we are disobedient children.
>
> —FREDERICK DENISON MAURICE

79

have since returned, I want you to stand." Dozens of people of all ages, from young adults like me to senior citizens, stood up. "Moms, dads," he said, "there's your hope."

Oh, my. What happened next pretty much put an end to church as we knew it that day. Each returned prodigal found a grieving parent to hug and cry with and quietly encourage. Words proved to be completely unnecessary. Our pastor had gotten that powerful demonstration of hope he so desperately wanted for his congregation.

I don't know if that verse in Proverbs is a promise or a principle. Furthermore, I don't particularly care. What I know is this: I had a mother who prayed for me and never gave up hope that I would change my evil ways and return to the household of faith. And for years she had nothing tangible to pin her hopes on, not one iota of evidence that I would ever trade in my life of diminished possibilities for a life of promise. I had rejected God and, even worse, believed God had rejected me; I mocked Christians and scorned the Scriptures. And yet I returned, just like the prodigal son that Jesus taught about in Luke 15:11–32, one of my favorite passages of the Scriptures I no longer scorn.

Your prodigal children never stop being your children, no matter what they do. And they never stop being sons and daughters of God, no matter what they do. If you continue to love them no matter what they do, imagine how much more God loves them no matter what they do. God's love has the advantage of being a lot more powerful than yours. Think about it: the love of the God I thought had rejected me is so

Just as you who were at one time disobedient to God have now received mercy as a result of their disobedience, so they too have now become disobedient in order that they too may now receive mercy as a result of God's mercy to you.

—ROMANS 11:30–31 (NIV)

powerful that it broke through to me even though I barely even believed that God existed. That's what I call powerful.

Look around you. You may not know it, but your life is very likely populated with plenty of returned prodigals. They are your hope.

REFLECTION

A few months ago I visited a small church called the Chapel of the Prodigal at the beautiful Montreat College in the mountains of North Carolina near Asheville. The chapel features a stunning fresco, *Return of the Prodigal* by Ben Long. As I alternately sat and stood during the service I attended there, I could not take my eyes off the painting, which I think is the point. I decided right then that there was no way on earth I would ever tire of reading or hearing the parable of the prodigal son.

There are several sites on the Internet where you can view the fresco, but the images are much too small to appreciate. You'll just have to go to Montreat to see it in its full-size glory. In lieu of that, following the example of theological reflection in the previous chapter, read the parable of the prodigal son in Luke 15:11–32 and place yourself in the role that most accurately reflects who you are today or, perhaps, who you were at one time: the joyous father, the jealous brother, the returned prodigal. Imagine the parable played out with you in that role, and pay attention to the insights you glean from the exercise.

> Love begins as love for one or for a few. But once we have caught it, once we have taken possession of it, and it has set up its own values in the heart of the self, there are no limits to those it can touch, to the relationships which it can transform.
>
> —JOHN AUSTIN BAKER

PRACTICE

We don't know from the biblical text of the parable of the prodigal son whether the father had lost all hope that his son would return; he says the boy had been given up for dead, but I wonder. I suspect he was like most people; without evidence, without proof, wouldn't we still hold out hope that our loved one was still alive? One thing we do know: the son had some measure of hope, however small, that his father would forgive him. Look what happens when he approaches his father's farm:

> When he was still a long way off, his father saw
> him. His heart pounding, he ran out, embraced him,
> and kissed him. The son started his speech: "Father,
> I've sinned against God, I've sinned before you; I
> don't deserve to be called your son ever again." But
> the father wasn't listening. He was calling to the ser-
> vants, "Quick. Bring a clean set of clothes and dress
> him. Put the family ring on his finger and sandals
> on his feet." (Luke 15:20–22, *The Message*)

To me, the overarching message of this parable is that some-times we are forgiven before we even ask, which means we, in turn, need to forgive even if our offender hasn't asked us to. Make this your practice: forgive those who have offended you, especially those who feel they have no hope of deserving your forgiveness. The more often you forgive, the easier it gets.

Cultivating a Hopeful Spirit

When you choose hope, anything's possible.
—Christopher Reeve

One bad call. That's all it took to dismantle my hopes for a career as a professional tennis player. Well, that and the fact that I didn't have much natural talent or the determination to compensate for that lack. But tennis was my sport of choice, if only for a few fleeting years. When my tennis coach disqualified one blissfully satisfying, match-winning stroke on the spurious basis that the ball had hit the ground before connecting with my racket, I lost it—"it" being both my objectivity and my status as a gracious loser.

I took to watching tennis from the sidelines of TV screens, which is where I first saw Andrea Jaeger play. As a young teenager, Andrea was a pioneer on the women's professional tennis circuit, turning pro at fourteen—old by today's standards—and ranking number two on the professional circuit by the age of sixteen. Within five years, though, a shoulder injury ended her career. For whatever reason—her youth, her signature pigtails,

If children have the ability to ignore all odds and percentages, then maybe we can all learn from them. When you think about it, what other choice is there but to hope? We have two options, medically and emotionally: give up, or fight like hell.

—LANCE ARMSTRONG

her spirit—I never forgot her, even years after she dropped out of the public eye.

Until 2004, I did not know what had become of Andrea. In the spring of that year, my editor at FaithfulReader.com asked me to interview her about the release of her book *First Service: Following God's Calling and Finding Life's Purpose.* Few interviews have impacted me the way that one did, wrapped as it was in an unimaginable measure of hope and joy in the face of equally unimaginable despair and sorrow. Andrea, as it turned out, had found a second and far more satisfying career ministering to cancer-stricken children by offering them the time of their lives in the Rockies.

From an early age, Andrea sensed that God had a purpose for her life beyond making a comfortable living and a name for herself. Even while she was on the pro circuit, she would take the time to visit children in hospitals, bringing them toys and leaving the media behind. These visits were no photo ops; they were Andrea's heartbeat.

With her career earnings—and the sale of some of her more valuable personal possessions—Andrea launched the Silver Lining Foundation in 1990 (now called Little Star Foundation). Several benefactors helped Jaeger realize her dream by donating land worth $10 million and a $1.7 million gift to build a lodge on the land. Today, the ten-acre Benedict-Forstmann Silver Lining Ranch in Aspen, Colorado, is a truly remarkable place where kids with cancer can stay for an expense-free, treatment-free, hospital-free week and rediscover the joy of just being kids once again.

Who would think of such a thing? Who would think to exchange an easy life for one filled with ailing children, many of them facing certain death in the near future? Who would think to offer those children an opportunity—quite possibly their last opportunity—for exuberance?

Only a person with a hopeful spirit.

And Andrea has that and then some.

After sixteen years in this venture, Andrea says she is just beginning to understand the depth of the lifelong ministry God has called her to. Several years into the work in Aspen, she realized that her involvement with each child who stayed at the ranch needed to continue for a lifetime—hers or theirs. "These kids make friends at the ranch, and then they see their friends leave them [when they die]," Andrea recently told me. "The ones who have been hurt the most will test you to no end to see if *you* will still be there for them." Andrea and three other women, including co-founder Heidi Bookout, have made a commitment to always be there for them.

But kids grow up, and the Silver Lining Foundation has learned to grow up with them. The Aspen ranch is now only one of dozens of projects that are part of the Little Star Foundation. Several years ago, the foundation purchased more than two hundred acres in the Durango, Colorado, area to start work on a second facility. When Rancho Milagro opens in 2007, it will function as a spiritual retreat center.

The work of the foundation extends far beyond the state boundaries of Colorado, by the way. Early on, it became evident

The most vital movement mortals feel is hope, the balm and lifeblood of the soul.

—JOHN ARMSTRONG

that many children would be unable to make the trip to Aspen, and so the Ranch on the Road program was born. Young cancer patients in a given area were treated to special events designed to accommodate their level of illness. The ranch program also headed for areas beyond the U.S. borders; the Little Star Foundation now offers programs for children around the world. Still, they've never forgotten the "kids"—now young adults—who first visited the Aspen facilities and who have survived cancer; the ranch regularly holds reunions for them, keeps in touch with them on holidays and birthdays, and has even helped put several through college courtesy of a scholarship fund that was started a number of years ago. In all, the ranch has five hundred children and young adults in its long-term cancer care program.

Does Andrea Jaeger possess a hopeful spirit? You bet she does. I can only imagine what it must be like devoting nearly every ounce of energy, every waking thought, every single day to cancer-stricken children, all of whom are certainly suffering and some of whom will die a very young death. It has to take an extraordinary measure of grace and an over-the-top measure of hope to push through the moments of despair and sorrow and grief that come with the life work Andrea has chosen—or perhaps better, the calling she has chosen to accept. There's no doubt that this is a calling. No one but God would ever ask such a thing of a human being. And no one but God could ever provide what it takes to live out such a calling.

The only disability in life is a bad attitude.

—SCOTT HAMILTON

REFLECTION

What is God's call on your life? Many people struggle with the idea of a calling. It sounds so lofty, so noble, so unlike their very ordinary lives. When Andrea Jaeger first started visiting children in hospitals, she had no idea that her life would be devoted to young cancer patients. She was simply doing what she sensed God wanted her to do at that time. Our calling is simply to do what we sense God wants us to do at a given time in our lives. The vast majority of us will never be called to a ministry like Andrea has today, but every one of us has a calling that is tailor made for our personalities, our circumstances, our talents. If you have no idea what your calling is, think about the ways you serve other people—or would like to serve other people. That's where the heart of your calling is, though it can take on different forms. My calling, for example, is primarily as a writer, but knitting for charities, working with hospice patients, and speaking and teaching are all a part of God's call on my life. Once you've determined what your calling is, reflect on the role hope plays in your service to others.

> The greatest discovery of my generation is that a human being can alter his life by altering his attitudes.
>
> —WILLIAM JAMES

PRACTICE

Without giving it a whole lot of thought, quickly make a list of those things that either anger you or grieve you. Include everything from the mundane (dishonest mechanics) to the profound (the abuse of the elderly in nursing homes). Somewhere in that list you're bound to find your "heartbeat"—the ministry to which you are called. Maybe you'll discover that you're a crusader at heart, and you're ready to fight for nursing-home reform. Or maybe you'll realize that you've been called to serve the needy by volunteering to fix their cars. Both are valid callings. God will show you what calling is valid for you.

16

Going to Hell in a Handbasket

We are disillusioned because we've believed an illusion for
thirty-something years now.

—Gerald Mann

No one seems to have a definitive answer regarding the ori-
gin of the phrase "going to hell in a handbasket." But most people understand its meaning: things are going downhill, and
quickly. And many of those people believe that is exactly what
is happening in the world today, particularly in America. They
have little hope that humankind will survive the overwhelming
threats to its existence.

The picture appears to be a bleak one indeed. The preva-
lence of terrorism, war, and genocide provide sufficient evidence that people are capable of committing unthinkable acts
against other people. Our inability to stem the tide of disasters
such as hurricanes, earthquakes, and tsunamis leaves us feeling
helpless against the forces of nature. Debilitating disorders and
deadly diseases rob us of our hope for a vibrant and healthy
future. As I write this, the apparently viable threat of an
avian flu pandemic hangs over our heads. And despite the com-
bined efforts of governmental agencies, nonprofits, ministries,

Nothing worth doing is completed in our lifetime; therefore we must be saved by hope. Nothing true or beautiful makes complete sense in any immediate context of history; therefore we must be saved by faith. Nothing we do, however virtuous, can be accomplished alone; therefore, we are saved by love.

—REINHOLD NIEBUHR

missions, and private foundations, we barely make a dent in the walls of poverty that hold so many people captive.

Is the picture bleak? Yes—if all you can see in that picture is the darkness that surrounds us or the catastrophes that loom ahead of us. Is the situation hopeless? That depends on where your hope lies.

The threats are valid. The devastating impact of 9/11 and Hurricane Katrina, the war in Iraq and the 2004 tsunami in Indonesia, the "ethnic cleansing" in Darfur and the famine in much of East Africa have given substance to the worst fears of millions of people. Untold numbers of victims had placed their faith and trust in a God who would protect them and rescue them from disaster. Still they died. Or they suffered. Or they watched their loved ones suffer and die.

There's more, much more. I've barely scratched the surface. It's not surprising, I suppose, that for as long as I can remember, I've heard people say that they wouldn't want to bring a child into a world like this, and so they choose to remain childless. Many who have brought children into a world like this fret over the future those children face.

Behind all this is the nagging feeling that by now we—the entire human race—should be better off than we are. We should be kinder and gentler and better able to resolve the conflicts that threaten to tear the world apart. We should have the answers to war and poverty and disease. We should have better systems in place to warn people about impending disaster and better methods of assisting people when disaster strikes.

What this means is that many people are plagued not only by

a personal sense of despair arising out of a particular situation but also by a collective feeling of hopelessness arising out of the global situation—the sorry state the world is in. And in their estimation, things can only get worse.

Gerald Mann's perspective on this feeling of universal hopelessness closely resembles my own. Especially in America, we have become disillusioned because we have believed an illusion. He limits the life of that illusion to the last thirty or so years, but I suspect the illusion has been a part of the fabric of American life ever since the Puritans thought they could create a better life in the New World. In my own lifetime, people have believed—and in some cases, I have also believed—that we could actually end poverty and discrimination, put a stop to unjust wars, find a cure for cancer, and even control weather patterns to avert natural calamities.

Which brings us right back to God, because that's who we think we are whenever we entertain the notion that we are ultimately in control. It's not a conscious thought, but our actions betray our subconscious thinking that we can change human nature—the force behind our social ills—or suddenly change the course of disease and disaster. (I have far greater hope in the latter; I have no doubt we'll find a cure for cancer long before we find a cure for discrimination.)

The illusion that humanity is evolving into a higher, nobler version of itself has evaporated. We are left with the raw reality of our frailties and limitations. We feel helpless in the face of the enormous problems that plague our society and the rest of the world.

But wait. Our problems are played out on a global stage; we know more about those problems because we have access to news and information as no previous generation has. Throughout recorded history, though, some of the world's greatest thinkers have prophesied the end of civilization—the end of humanity, even—because of the bleak picture of the future that they created from their present. And every one of those great thinkers has been wrong, because they failed to include the concept of hope in the pictures they painted.

Some credit the survival of civilization to the resilience of the human spirit, and I have no doubt that our ability to bounce back from defeat and hardship is a critical factor in keeping humanity alive on Earth. But I also know this: the human spirit in all its resiliency is not enough. Only when it is joined with the Spirit of God does the human spirit have what it takes to keep going and keep believing despite the many evidences of doom and gloom that join forces in an attempt to rid the world of all traces of hope.

Going to hell in a handbasket? I don't think so. When we recognize our limitations and acknowledge our lack of control over so much in life, we find ourselves in the humbling position of admitting that our only lasting hope is in God. God alone gives us the eyes to see the hope that is missing from the bleakest pictures.

REFLECTION

U.S. Army General Robert E. Lee once said, "It is history that teaches us to hope." Never mind that he came in second in

> If we were logical, the future would be bleak indeed. But we are more than logical. We are human beings, and we have faith and we have hope, and we can work.
>
> —JACQUES COUSTEAU

the War of Northern Aggression. (Can you tell I was born in the South?) If we only look at the current state of the world, we have no real context for hope. We need to understand how far humanity has come—against overwhelming odds—in order to build up a supply of reasons to have hope for the future. If you include the Black Plague in that supply, well, you're pretty much home free.

But back to the good general. Do you believe that history teaches us to hope—or at least contributes to our ability to hope? If not, why not? What is it about human history that contributes to a sense of despair—the sense that the world is going to hell in a handbasket? Do you think your hope would be strengthened by a greater appreciation for the catastrophes, both natural and manmade, that humanity has survived throughout recorded history?

PRACTICE

Blog. Blog about your concerns, your fears, your hopes for the world. Tell everyone you know, and lots of people you don't know, about your blog. Blogging, or keeping a weblog, is a great way to clarify your thoughts, and since it's public, your blog may invite others to join in the conversation. Who knows? You and your circle may discover the way to world peace! And even if you don't, at least you've given yourself an opportunity to express your thoughts and feelings.

It is history that teaches us to hope.

—ROBERT E. LEE

17

The Hope of Depression

Even the cry from the depths is an affirmation; why cry
if there is no hint of hope of hearing?
—Martin Marty

Few people, I'm sure, would ever think of hope in the same
context as depression. Although the clinical cause of chronic
depression is often stated as anger turned inward, hopelessness
is certainly a factor in its diagnosis. Author William Styron,
who wrote *Sophie's Choice* and *The Confessions of Nat Turner*
among other marvelous books, expressed the despair that
accompanies depression in this way:

> In depression this faith in deliverance, in ultimate
> restoration, is absent. The pain is unrelenting, and
> what makes the condition intolerable is the fore-
> knowledge that no remedy will come—not in a day,
> an hour, a month, or a minute.… It is hopelessness
> even more than pain that crushes the soul. So the
> decision making of daily life involves not, as in nor-
> mal affairs, shifting from one annoying situation to
> another less annoying—from discomfort to relative

comfort, or from boredom to activity—but moving from pain to pain. One does not abandon, even briefly, one's bed of nails, but is attached to it wherever one goes.[15]

The phrase most striking to me in Styron's description of the hopelessness of depression is "the foreknowledge that no remedy will come." That's a vitally important insight for those who live or work with a depressed person to understand. You cannot convince a clinically depressed person that "this too shall pass"; it's pointless to try. You cannot expect a depressed person to have faith in either deliverance or restoration; in fact, you cannot expect a depressed person to have faith at all, regardless of how strong his faith may have been at an earlier point in his life. You can also forget about suggesting that the person pray or read the Bible or get out of bed and go to church or other services or "Just start singing praise songs to God!"—which was what one well-intentioned but clueless person prescribed for me when I was utterly paralyzed by depression.

During my time of emotional paralysis, I knew without a doubt there would be no relief from the pain I was in. The way life was for me then was the way life would always be. And God? The God I had tried to love and serve for all of my adult life was nowhere to be found, and I had long since given up looking. I stubbornly refused to acknowledge that I had anything to do with the fact that we had parted ways. God had abandoned me, and that was that. End of story. Except that the story kept going, day after endless day. I hated my life and I

In the midst of winter, I found there was, within me, an invincible summer.

—ALBERT CAMUS

hated myself for hating my life, because I knew deep down I had a good life. That just made things worse. Since I couldn't appreciate the good life I had, well, that just proved there was no hope for me. As it did with William Styron, hopelessness was crushing my soul.

We were in good company, though, Styron and I. King David also knew deep depression. Here's how he described his despair:

> My whole body is sick.... My wounds fester and stink.... I am bent over and racked with pain. My days are filled with grief. A raging fever burns within me, and my health is broken. I am exhausted and completely crushed. My groans come from an anguished heart.... My heart beats wildly, my strength fails, and I am going blind. My loved ones and friends stay away, fearing my disease. Even my own family stands at a distance.... I am on the verge of collapse, facing constant pain. (Excerpts from Ps. 38:3–17, NLT)

From the context of this psalm, we know that the physical symptoms David describes, such as the festering wounds, were a result of his depression and not the cause of it. He was in such despair that his health was, as he put it, broken. Even so, David had one major advantage over me: though he didn't sense God's immediate presence, neither did he believe that God had abandoned him yet: "I am waiting for you, O Lord. You must

How very good it is when you can awaken your heart and plead to God until tears stream from your eyes, and you stand like a little child crying to its parent.

—Rebbe Nachman of Breslov

answer for me, O Lord my God…. Do not abandon me, Lord. Do not stand at a distance, my God. Come quickly to help me, O Lord my savior" (verses 15, 21–22). His was not a depression characterized by hopelessness; I have to wonder what today's mental health practitioners would make of him and his symptoms. Perhaps they'd say he was depressed, but not clinically so.

David's psalm shows that it's possible to be depressed and still have hope. But for people whose experiences differ dramatically from his, there is still a connection between depression and hope. That connection comes when you finally realize and admit that you're suffering from depression—because then, there's hope not only of overcoming the depression itself but also of altering those elements in your life that contributed to the depression in the first place.

Unless it's precipitated by a single traumatic event, such as the death of a loved one, depression can be a long time in the making. Looking back over my own life, I can now recognize myriad factors that built upon each other to bring me to the brink of despair. But because it happened over such a long period of time, my descent into the abyss of depression was a gradual one; I did not know what was happening to me until it was too late—too late in the sense that I could not emerge from it without taking medication to restore a normal brain chemistry, and then begin to make changes in my lifestyle and my way of thinking.

Once the medication kicked in, "the foreknowledge that no remedy [would] come" simply disappeared. I began to sense that I was getting better, and hope began to play a significant role in my recovery. Though I'll never forget what it felt like to experience the hopelessness of depression, I have to work at consciously remembering the excruciating pain I was in. Today, I can hardly imagine living without hope.

God had not abandoned me; I was just too sick to sense his presence. I had convinced myself that God had been out to get me, and when he did—when he made sure I was an emotional wreck—then he up and left me. Once my brain started functioning normally again, I was able to see the fallacy in that way of thinking, and my faith in God's constant presence in my life was fully restored. My life today is brimming over with hope.

I periodically thank God for my depression. I'm sure that makes no sense to some people, but others understand how and why I can do that. Depression is like physical pain in that it alerts us to the fact that something is terribly wrong with us. If we never felt the pain of a toothache, for instance, we probably wouldn't have any teeth left. If I had never suffered the pain of depression, my tendency toward workaholism may have cost me everything, including my family. I may have continued in a job and in a ministry that I was ill suited for. And I may have maintained one very faulty perception of God's grace and love and mercy.

Yes, there is a connection between hope and depression—a very strong and healthy one. It's a connection that can result in lasting, positive changes in our lives.

REFLECTION

Meditate on Psalm 42 (in the New Living Translation below):

As the deer pants for streams of water, so I long for you, O God.

I thirst for God, the living God. When can I come and stand before him?

Day and night, I have only tears for food, while my enemies continually taunt me, saying, "Where is this God of yours?"

My heart is breaking as I remember how it used to be: I walked among the crowds of worshipers, leading a great procession to the house of God, singing for joy and giving thanks—it was the sound of a great celebration!

Why am I discouraged? Why so sad? I will put my hope in God! I will praise him again—my Savior and my God!

Now I am deeply discouraged, but I will remember your kindness—from Mount Hermon, the source of the Jordan, from the land of Mount Mizar.

I hear the tumult of the raging seas as your waves and surging tides sweep over me.

Through each day the Lord pours his unfailing love upon me, and through each night I sing his songs, praying to God who gives me life.

"O God my rock," I cry, "why have you forsaken me? Why must I wander in darkness, oppressed by my enemies?"

Their taunts pierce me like a fatal wound. They scoff, "Where is this God of yours?"

Why are you downcast, O my soul? Why so disturbed within me? Put your hope in God, for I will yet praise him, my Savior and my God.

—PSALM 42:5–6 (NIV)

Why am I discouraged? Why so sad? I will put my hope in God! I will praise him again—my Savior and my God!

PRACTICE

Learn all you can about depression. Maybe you've never suffered from it, and I hope you never will, but you do know, have known, and will know people who are clinically depressed. The more you understand it, the more hope you can offer to those who suffer from it. What's more, when you know the symptoms, you're more likely to recognize them in yourself if they begin to creep into your life. One of the best places to start is with the National Institute of Mental Health (www.nimh.nih.gov); there are many other sites and organizations, but you have to be careful where you get your information. Many health and mental illness sites are sponsored by pharmaceutical and health supplement companies; many provide very good information, but it's important to keep in mind that they are businesses and not governmental or nonprofit organizations. Other good resources are the many books on depression written from a faith-based perspective.

Please don't ignore this practice. You have no idea today how valuable it may be to you and your loved ones in the future.

I never knew God lived so close to the floor.

—SHEILA WALSH, DESCRIBING HER STRUGGLE WITH DEPRESSION

The God Who Loves Us

God's will is not an itinerary, but an attitude.

—Andrew Dhuse

One of the saddest episodes during my on-again, off-again relationship with church did so much damage to so many people that some walked away from God completely and never looked back. The problem started when our pastor fell under the spell of some well-meaning but seriously misguided nationally known leaders. The end result was nothing short of the transformation of our local congregation into a cult. Topping the list of egregious abuses committed in the name of Jesus was spiritual manipulation.

Like most cults, this one began to take root so subtly that at first only a few people noticed. I was happily distracted by other things—love and marriage and a baby carriage, to name a few—and so I remained oblivious to the seriousness of the problem for far too long. There were a lot of rumors flying around, too, and I really, really despise rumors. The church was well into theological error before I came up for air and could finally see the devastation these "leaders" had caused. When I did, it was through the eyes of a sweet young woman who loved God too much for her own good. Jeri—not her real name— loved God so much that she readily believed everything she heard, as long as it came from the mouth of someone else who also presumably loved God. Her unquestioning trust in all things labeled "Christian" prevented her from practicing spiritual discernment.

I didn't know Jeri all that well, but I sensed she was emotionally fragile and a bit naïve. Still, I liked her and had always enjoyed her company. One afternoon she stopped by to visit a friend of hers whom I happened to also be visiting. That was the day my eyes were finally opened to the tragedy unfolding at the church. Because Jeri's husband was a friend of the pastor's, she was privy to a great deal that I knew nothing about. At the time, our church was planning a series of meetings featuring one of the leaders, who by then had become something of a celebrity. He and his entourage told her husband that they would only grace us with their presence if every member of the church was "right with God"—that is, praying faithfully for the success of the meetings and being fully supportive of the leader's teachings. "Just think!" Jeri said. "Any one of us could keep this whole thing from happening! I don't want it to be my fault! I made sure I got right with God last night!" She did not know how to talk about her faith without using an abundance of exclamation marks.

Right then and there, I saw the light—and I don't mean the light of God. I saw that the spotlight had been taken off God and placed on this leader and his minions, my pastor included.

A sober, devout man will interpret "God's will" soberly and devoutly. A fanatic, with bloodshot mind, will interpret "God's will" fanatically. Men of extreme, illogical views will interpret "God's will" in eccentric fashion. Kindly, charitable, generous men will interpret "God's will" according to their character.

—E. HALDEMAN-JULIUS

And they were getting people like Jeri to do their bidding by couching their demands in ominous religious terms. Jeri became so fearful of doing or saying the wrong thing, and so obsessed with following the "perfect will of God," that she eventually had a breakdown from which she has never recovered.

Our little church was only one of hundreds that fell prey to the machinations of a few power-hungry men. They had people believing that they needed to pray to discover this ever-elusive "perfect will of God" in everything they did—selecting the clothes to wear to work, choosing the route to take to work, deciding where to go for lunch, every blessed little thing in their blessed little lives. The danger in not seeking God's will in everything was obvious: If you failed to pray about where to eat lunch, you might go to the wrong restaurant and miss meeting the one person in the world that God had hand-picked to be your spouse. Then where would you be? You would be relegated to a life of—horrors!—singleness or forced to marry someone who was only second best.

Poet Carl Dennis must have visited my church at some point during that time. Surely my church was the inspiration for his poem "The God Who Loves You," which is part of a collection titled *Practical Gods* that won him the Pulitzer Prize in 2002. In it, he portrays a worried, fretful God who grieves over the choices you've made in life (the poem is addressed directly to "you," the reader). Those choices were all second best; if only you had gone to a different college, for example, your roommate there would have inspired you to pursue the genuine passion of your soul, assuring that you would not have settled for the mundane career you have today. What's more, you missed out on meeting the love of your life at that other school; now you're stuck in a relationship that satisfies neither of you. God knew the path you should have taken, and it saddens God that you took the wrong one.

It's fascinating to me that some readers interpret the poem as an indictment of God; if only God would speak up, we would make all the right choices. I'm guessing those readers never attended a truly dysfunctional, controlling church or never bought into the fundamentalist Christian teaching on God's perfect will. Many of us who did attend such a church and did buy into such a doctrine believed that God had custom-designed exactly one path for each of us, and it was our responsibility to discover God's perfect will for our lives. That discovery came at a high cost, literally; we spent our money on books, tapes, seminars, and entire conferences devoted to finding God's will for our lives. Since no two leaders seemed to offer the same teaching, our bank accounts were quickly drained. We couldn't afford to miss that one teaching that would help us figure out how to determine God's will.

For some people, the prescription to seek God's perfect will provides the perfect setup for a life without hope. What kind of hope can we possibly have if we believe that God has carefully mapped out one future for us and one future only—and then requires us to spend all our time trying to find out exactly what that future is? Our lives would end up riddled with fear—the fear that if we made one wrong move, just one misstep, we would throw off the whole plan.

That's no way to live. I'll take my life as it is and forgo the temptation to question whether it was God's perfect will, whether I got it right or not. This is the life I've chosen; so be it.

REFLECTION

What do you really believe about God's involvement in your life? Do you see God as a great chess master, moving this piece over there and that piece to the spot just vacated and so on? As a stern taskmaster, watching your every move to see just how badly you're going to mess up the job you've been given to do? As a kindly old gentleman who winks his eye at you when you misbehave? As a mother wrapping her children in a warm embrace of love? Move away from stereotypes and toward a fresh and original picture of God that has a special and unique meaning to you.

PRACTICE

I've said this before, and I'll keep on saying it: church drives me crazy. And yet, I believe that involvement in a community of faith is so valuable that I will never give up on it. Which puts me in quite a dilemma: do I walk away from church and lose my faith, or stay in church and lose my mind? Oh, the challenges.

What about your community of faith? Sometimes, due to geographical restrictions or the limited number of like-minded

God guides us first through his Word, then through our heartfelt desires, then the wise counsel of others, and then our circumstances. At that point we must rely on our own sound judgment.... God gave each of us a brain, and he expects us to put it to good use.

—BRUCE K. WALTKE

The fact that I think that I am following your will does not mean that I am actually doing so. But I believe that the desire to please you does in fact please you.

—Thomas Merton

faithful in a given area, we have little choice about where we worship. But we can dream, no?

Start by creating your dream community of faith. List the elements you hunger for in worship services and other aspects of congregational life. Because I'm Christian, my list includes the centrality of Jesus, a deep commitment to the value of the Scriptures and other spiritual writings, respect for the wisdom of the ages and other faiths, an openness to anyone and everyone, opportunity for everyone to contribute through teaching, service, ministry, and so forth. (My list is too long to reproduce here, which may be why I have such a hard time with church.)

Now that you've created your dream community and you realize you'll never find one that remotely resembles it, start a second list—those things you may not be crazy about but that you know you can tolerate. One of the things on my list, for example, would be aesthetics. If I had my way I'd live close enough to some great English Gothic cathedral where I could worship, but I'd also worship in a storefront if it meant I'd found an authentic community of faith.

List number three: what you absolutely will not tolerate. I wish I'd made this list years ago, when I decided to overlook certain mediocre aspects of the worship service at one church. I stayed for three years, during which I heard certain sermons a half-dozen or more times. It got so bad that I was preaching the sermon in my head along with the pastor, anecdotes and illustrations and not-so-funny jokes and all. If I had trusted my instincts and admitted to myself that I wouldn't be able to handle that particular problem, I would have spared myself and others a lot of sadness when I finally realized I had to leave.

Keep the items on your list firmly in mind. It may explain why you're unhappy where you are—or why you're blissfully content there. And if you ever move, you'll have a clear idea of what you want to look for.

19

Drama 101

We are faced with a decision that grows with urgency each passing day: Will we leave our small stories behind and venture forth to follow our Beloved into the Sacred Romance? The choice to become a pilgrim of the heart can happen any day, and we can begin our journey from any place.

—Brent Curtis and John Eldredge

To look at me today, it's difficult to imagine that I was once quite the backpacking buff. The thought of either component of that compound noun—"back" and "packing"—creates an immediate image of pain these days. But before my body up and betrayed me, I spent most of my vacations and many a long weekend hiking on various portions of the Appalachian Trail. Everything about backpacking stirred my heart and soul: the challenge of the trail's terrain, the constant need for vigilance, the element of risk, the knowledge that the whole experience could be a wonder—or a disaster. Even before setting out, I enjoyed something of a masochistic pleasure in reducing the weight of my pack by one more ounce, and then another and another; trimming down my needs for survival on a hike provided a perfect foil for the clutter in the rest of my life.

On every hike, there were always at least two moments of absolute bliss. One was the exquisite pleasure of sliding into a sleeping bag; dirty, sweaty, muscles aching, joints resisting movement, an overlooked stone under the tent floor poking my back—none of that mattered. Horizontal never feels so good as it does on the trail.

The second moment often occurred at dusk, when it was time to pitch the tent and fix dinner and get ready for that horizontal moment. That's when I would take a breather, find a quiet spot, and just *be* for a while. Those were moments of indescribable beauty, despite the weather, despite the discomfort, despite the creepy-crawlies about. I was at peace with God and the world, if only for a few moments.

One evening on the Virginia portion of the Appalachian Trail, my husband and I finished dinner at our campsite and walked a mile or so to an overlook we had passed along the way. In the valley below, the lights of the city of Luray were just beginning to twinkle; behind the mountains to the west, the setting sun was just barely visible. Everything seemed blanketed in a thin veil of lavender. We sat on the ground for who knows how long, not saying a word to each other. To speak, I'm sure, would have been a transgression, a corruption of a beautiful and haunting moment, a moment as close to perfection as I'll ever know on earth.

It's in moments like that one, authors Brent Curtis and John Eldredge believe, that we catch a glimpse of the eternal drama unfolding behind the scenes of our lives. They call this drama "the Sacred Romance," which is also the title of a book in which

There is surely a future hope for you, and your hope will not be cut off.

—Proverbs 23:18

(NIV)

they portray life as God's invitation to pursue beauty, intimacy, and adventure—and a love relationship with the Spirit.

> The desire God has placed within us is wild in its longing to pursue the One who is unknown. Its capacity and drive is so powerful that it can only be captured momentarily in moments of deep soul communion or sexual ecstasy. And when the moment has passed, we can only hold it as an ache, a haunting of quicksilver that flashes a remembrance of innocence known and lost and, if we have begun to pass into the life of the Beloved, a hope of ecstasies yet to come.... It strikes us that to hope in the kind of goodness that would set our heart free, we must be willing to allow our desire to remain haunted.[16]

Everybody needs beauty as well as bread, places to play in and pray in, where nature may heal and cheer and give strength to body and soul alike.

—JOHN MUIR

Those haunting moments last just long enough to convince us that we were made for much more than the surface of our lives indicates; we were created to play a part in the eternal drama Eldredge and Curtis describe. In this drama, every one of us has a role, even if it's the role of an understudy. Our seemingly small and insignificant lives have purpose and meaning and greatness and significance. We're part of a story that has been unfolding throughout human history.

Because this drama ultimately exists beyond the limitations of time, it's hard for us to get a handle on what our role is in the here-and-now. But we can hold on to "a future hope" (Prov. 23:18), a time when the curtains will part and we'll be able to see the performance in its entirety, our role and all.

Our longings and yearnings for something more are not mere fantasies; they express our deepest needs, the secret desires of our heart that we push down further and further with every duty, every obligation, and every responsibility that robs us of experiencing beauty and intimacy and adventure. As Eldredge and Curtis put it, we've lost touch with our heart. But the good news is that all is not lost; we have the hope of restoration.

Our hope lies in the knowledge that we're not alone in wanting that restoration to take place. Even God is sick of our religiosity—our unbalanced lives of duty and obligation and responsibility: "These people come near to me with their mouth and honor me with their lips, but their hearts are far from me. Their worship of me is made up only of rules taught by men" (Isa. 29:13, NIV). God wants our hearts to be in touch with his heart. But here's the good part—God can restore our hearts and even promises to do so: "I will give you a new heart and put a new spirit in you; I will remove from you your heart of stone and give you a heart of flesh" (Ezek. 36:26, NIV). That's the hope we have—that our hearts can beat with the promise of beauty and intimacy and adventure, the heartbeat of a sacred romance.

REFLECTION

Here's a reflection straight from the heart and mind of John Eldredge:

> They who dwell in the ends of the earth stand in awe of Your signs; You make the dawn and the sunset shout for joy.
>
> **—PSALM 65:8 (NAS)**

Think of times in your life that made you wish for all the world that you had the power to make time stand still.... Something in your heart says, *Finally—it has come. This is what I was made for!*[17]

Do that. Think of those times. And then reflect on these questions: What exactly has come? What is it that you were made for?

PRACTICE

Find a place where you can just *be*. Outside, in a natural environment, is best, but I realize that's easier for some people than for others. I live in an area that some people consider paradise, but I can assure you that I will not *be* in the hot, humid, and pest-ridden wilds of Florida anytime between April and November. March and December are iffy, too. And February. January 10 is a good bet. Maybe. In the cool of the evening, though. Anyway, if you live in a city or some godforsaken swamp, do your best. Be creative.

But back to our exercise. Just *be*. No conscious thinking, no trying to problem-solve, no list making. It may take more than a few minutes to settle your mind and your spirit so you can just exist, but it is possible. Stay in that state for as long as possible. You'll know when it's time to return to reality. Just don't rush it.

Then go out and *be* again. Tomorrow, if possible.

The most beautiful thing we can experience is the mysterious. It is the source of all art and science. He to whom this emotion is a stranger, who can no longer pause to wonder and stand rapt in awe, is as good as dead; his eyes are closed.

—ALBERT EINSTEIN

20

The Persecuted Faithful

To suffer is beautiful. It hurts your body but fortifies your spirit.

—Domingo Lopez, persecuted pastor in Mexico

In the years I spent as an editor at *Charisma* magazine, my eyes were opened to the plight of persecuted believers around the world. Having come from a rural area with lousy radio reception and two and a half television stations—I'm not kidding—in the days before the Internet, I knew next to nothing about religious groups that faced ongoing persecution. It wasn't the kind of news that print journalists regularly reported on back then; the Internet has changed that situation dramatically, because now journalists face the prospect of being scooped or upstaged by real people disseminating real information about real crises in the world.

Today I couldn't avoid the news about the persecuted faithful even if I wanted to. My inbox is periodically inundated with updates about kidnappings, beatings, and murders primarily targeting Christians, since Christianity is the focus of most of my reporting. We know, of course, that other faith groups face equally severe persecution. For every target of persecution there's at least one totally useless Internet petition circling the globe over and over again. (We all do know that they're useless, right? That the intended final recipients—be they members of Congress, the president, or other world leaders—are also smart enough to know that they're useless, right? That the computers of the intended final recipients auto-delete them, right? Then why am I still getting them?)

Occasionally, I learn of these atrocities through personal contact. That was the case in 2005 when I became acquainted with Jacob Chinnappa, who owns a Christian publishing company in Hyderabad, India. I met Jacob less than two months after his pastor had been found dead on the side of a road. Pastor Daniel's face and body were so badly decomposed that he could only be identified through bits of his clothing and his unusual mobile phone strap. A Hindu extremist group called the Anti-Christian Forum claimed responsibility for Daniel's murder—and the subsequent mutilation and murder of another pastor two weeks later—in a letter to a local newspaper. Both men had been lured to a remote area by someone requesting a pastor to perform a wedding, and both had been garroted. When a suspect was finally identified and arrested, police learned that the killer had planned the murders of five more pastors.

If the Anti-Christian Forum expected the murders, and the threat of more murders, to force Christians into fleeing or hiding, their plan backfired. A year later, church involvement and membership had increased considerably—and inexplicably. Inexplicably, that is, unless you factor in the element of hope. Following the murders, pastors took greater care when they

> Understanding brings an awareness of the complexity [of religious persecution], complexity brings humility, humility brings discernment; discernment brings effectiveness.
>
> —RONALD BOYD-MACMILLAN

traveled, especially when they had to go from village to village on the outskirts of major cities, but they did not give up their hope. They proceeded with caution whenever a stranger called asking for assistance, but they did not give up their hope. They provided as much protection as they possibly could during house-church meetings, but they did not give up their hope. Hope that flourishes despite extreme adversity becomes a powerful magnet, and that was the case with the visible hope of the persecuted Christians in India.

Ronald Boyd-MacMillan, author of *Faith That Endures,* credits extremism itself with causing the churches to grow, citing among other things a conversation he had with a Dalit woman. Dalits are "untouchables," members of the lowest strata in India's four-level caste system. Look at what she said:

> I would never have become a Christian had the leaders of Hinduism not urged us to hate and kill, because it made me realize anew that they just wanted to keep me in the trap of my caste. They want me to stay untouchable so they can look down on me. When they started attacking the Christians, I said to myself, *I better find out what it is about Christianity that annoys them. If it annoys them, it may satisfy me.*[18]

My purpose in recounting this incident is not to paint a "Hindu bad/Christian good" picture; it's to emphasize that there is hope in even the worst situations we can find ourselves in. I'm sure many of the Christians in the villages surrounding Hyderabad feared for their lives, and some no doubt gave up hope altogether. But as their numbers began to strengthen, and as the news of their persecution attracted the attention of people of all faiths, the local police and government began to feel the pressure to correct the injustices. Although they have a long way to go—extremists aren't all that easily subdued—Christians are slowly, very slowly, gaining a greater degree of respect and recognition on a political level in and around Hyderabad than they had before, though the same is not necessarily true in other parts of India.

The irony is this: the persecuted faithful are so much more *faithful* than the rest of us. I have never read or heard anything that suggests otherwise. They cram more Scripture into their heads in a year than many of us do in a lifetime, because they know their Bibles could be confiscated or stolen at any moment. They pray more frequently and fervently than most of us do, because they *need* to pray more frequently and fervently. And they have more hope than we have, because that's about all they have.

REFLECTION

Domingo Lopez is a pastor in the state of Chiapas in Mexico, where money-hungry *caciques,* political bosses who control the local economy, routinely persecute evangelical Christians. Why? Because the Christians don't drink alcohol, which is very, very bad for business. Furthermore, the *caciques* demand that

Tolerance implies no lack of commitment to one's own beliefs. Rather it condemns the oppression or persecution of others.

—JOHN F. KENNEDY

everyone, including Christians, buy artifacts used in pagan sacrifices and rituals—at outrageously inflated prices. Some thirty-five thousand Christians have been driven off their land in Chiapas. And yet, Lopez calls suffering for God "beautiful." How can suffering be considered beautiful? Meditate on the concept of the beauty of suffering.

PRACTICE

Find out how you can help the persecuted faithful around the world. (Hint: It won't involve an e-mailed petition.) One of the features of Boyd-MacMillan's book that I appreciate the most is a three-chapter section on helping the persecuted, particularly one titled "The Tricky Business of Doing More Harm than Good." He writes: "In reality, helping the persecuted is messy, controversial, and confusing." He cautions against falling for methods that sound good and may give you the satisfaction of knowing you've done *something,* but they may be exactly the wrong things to do.

One of the best sources of information on religious persecution is Open Doors International, the organization with which Boyd-MacMillan is affiliated (which is why I trust what he has written). You can acquire an impressive education by roaming around their website, www.opendoorsusa.org. Other organizations include Voice of the Martyrs (www.persecution.com), International Christian Concern (www.persecution.org), and International Day of Prayer for the Persecuted Church (www.persecutedchurch.org), which provides links on its home

> Blessed are you when people insult you, persecute you and falsely say all kinds of evil against you because of me.... But I tell you: Love your enemies and pray for those who persecute you.
>
> —MATTHEW 5:11, 44 (NIV)

117

page to a dozen similar organizations. Within Reform Judaism, the Union of American Hebrew Congregations and the Central Conference of American Rabbis have spearheaded an effort to fight religious persecution, regardless of the particular religion that's being targeted; a good source of information on this movement is the Religious Action Center of Reform Judaism (www.rac.org).

We must shift our interest from the seen to the unseen. For the great unseen Reality is God.

—A. W. TOZER

21

Passing It On

Hope is like a road in the country; there never was a road,
but when many people walk on it, the road comes into
existence.

—Lin Yutang

When I think back to people who have given me hope, I
realize that what they gave me first was a different gift, but one
that is essential if we are to become hopeful: the gift of peace.
Think about that as it pertains to your own life; have you ever
known an optimistic person who did not have peace of mind?
I've become convinced that if we are to pass along a spirit of
hope to others, we need first to be at peace with ourselves, with
God, and, as much as possible, with the people in our lives.

During my frenetic days as a daily newspaper reporter, it
was understandably difficult to find either peace or hope. I was
generally a peaceful and hopeful person; the challenge was to
maintain that bearing in an environment replete with cynicism
and strife (the strife wasn't so much among staffers as it was
between reporters and the people they were reporting on; the
consequences of their conflicts eventually infiltrated the news-
room). Then I met a young couple whose names I've long since
forgotten. They were starting what was to be a loosely formed

community of prayer and fellowship; at the time I was religion editor at the *Asbury Park Press,* and what they were doing was unique enough to warrant a story.

I met with this couple in their home, and as soon as I entered, I felt different. I couldn't pin down what the feeling was at that moment; all I knew was that it had a calming effect on me. But I had a job to do, and I couldn't exactly get all mellow just then. As we talked, every so often I would think: "I want to be just like them." As I left their home, I felt as if everything in my life was going to be just fine even though we hadn't talked about me at all, nor did we talk about any deep issues that were of any concern to me. It wasn't until later that night when the dust from my day had settled that I was able to attach a word to my experience during the interview. The word was "peace." This couple had created such a peaceful atmosphere in their home and in their lives that it had rubbed off on me.

One of the reasons we may feel inadequate in our efforts to give other people hope is that we think we have to use words to do so, and words can sometimes sound glib or superficial or, even worse, preachy. We can communicate hope, however, in any number of ways, primarily by living our lives in accordance with our beliefs. If we truly have hope, then our lives should reflect our optimism. But as that young couple back in Asbury Park showed me, when we are at peace, we can help bring peace into the lives of others, and hope is sure to follow.

What if we don't have peace in our own lives? We don't have a prayer of passing on to others that which we don't have. For people of faith, restoring peace to our lives starts with our rela-

A mind at peace, a mind centered and not focused on harming others, is stronger than any physical force in the universe.

—WAYNE DYER

tionship with God. If that relationship isn't right, we need to get it right and begin to live in alignment with what we believe. In turn, we need to be in right relationship (again, as much as we can) with other people and get over whatever problems we have with ourselves. But that's a subject for another book.

Once you've read that other book, or gotten counseling or in some way come to terms with yourself, the best thing you can do to have peace of mind and a peaceful atmosphere in your home is to simplify. I know, I know—you can't. But you can. And if you start with that premise—that you can—and just pretend for a while that you really believe it, you may begin to identify, little by little, those possessions and activities that you can whittle away from your life.

I know how painful the thought of simplifying can be. It used to feel painful to me too. Then we had the fire I mentioned earlier—a "minor" electrical fire. The fire restoration crew packed up everything in our living room, dining area, kitchen, master bedroom, and closets, and either sent it out to be cleaned or cleaned it themselves and put it in storage. When we finally got back into the house after almost two months in a hotel, we faced the daunting task of unpacking. Four months later we're still not unpacked, and we aren't missing a single thing that's essential to our lives.

We're now opening one box at a time, when we have the time, taking out only things of sentimental value (our assessment of "sentimental value" has radically changed) and repacking the rest to donate to area charities. I used to treasure my book collection, which once contained three thousand volumes,

> Peace does not dwell in outward things, but within the soul; we may preserve it in the midst of the bitterest pain, if our will remains firm and submissive.
>
> —FRANÇOIS FENELON

but no more. When I realized that we would have lost everything if my husband had not been home when the fire broke out, simplifying became so much easier.

Ironically, I had already started the paring-down process right before the fire, motivated by what a friend of mine had experienced a few months earlier. She and her husband had both been in the military, and I used to be so envious of them every time they moved—they hardly had to lift a finger, even when they moved to and from Germany. The military packed everything for them and handled the entire move. But you know what happened? They never went through the winnowing process that most of us go through when we move, deciding what is really worth carting halfway across the country and what isn't. When Bob died, Alice faced the task of going through numerous file drawers of paperwork that needed to be shredded—and that was just the first step in reducing the stuff that had accumulated over twenty years of marriage.

Before Alice had regained the emotional strength she needed to start that project, she was diagnosed with cancer and had to begin chemo treatments, which zapped her of her physical strength. The unshredded documents awaiting her in those file cabinets increased her anxiety level considerably—and one thing she did not need was more cause for anxiety.

The fire taught me how little we need. Alice's predicament taught me that we need to simplify before circumstances prevent us from doing so. And both situations showed me that achieving peace in our lives is closely linked to our willingness and ability to simplify our lives. (A bonus benefit of simplifying

> In a world filled with causes for worry and anxiety ... we need the peace of God standing guard over our hearts and minds.
>
> —JERRY W. McCANT

is that it reduces our desires; after getting rid of so much, do we really want more stuff?)

When you start reducing your activities, keep—or add—some that involve genuine service to other people, something that will make a difference in their lives. Keep your thoughts and motives pure; keep your attachments to the things of this world to a minimum; and keep in mind your role in the larger story of life. All of those factors have helped me return to a more peaceful state when anxiety begins to creep in again.

REFLECTION

War and conflict throughout the world can rob us of our inner peace. Peace Pilgrim, the chosen name of a woman who logged more than twenty-five thousand miles on foot promoting peace at every level, made this observation about the relationship between inner peace and world peace:

> We can work on inner peace and world peace at the same time. On one hand, people have found inner peace by losing themselves in a cause larger than themselves, like the cause of world peace, because finding inner peace means coming from the self-centered life into the life centered in the good of the whole. On the other hand, one of the ways of working for world peace is to work for more inner peace, because world peace will never be stable until enough of us find inner peace to stabilize it.[19]

First keep peace with yourself, then you can also bring peace to others.

—THOMAS Á KEMPIS

Consider her thoughts from your own perspective. Do you believe that losing yourself in a larger cause would enhance your peace of mind or disturb it? When we get involved in a cause of any kind, we become better educated about the problems we're working to overcome. How can we guard against losing our peace as we discover more information about how overwhelming the problems are? How can we become more hopeful as a result?

PRACTICE

In the last thirty years of my church life I've seen a complete transformation in attitude toward meditation. In the 1970s, as forms of Eastern meditation became increasingly popular in the West, some church leaders cautioned against the practice of meditation in general. They feared that people would be led away from what they perceived as the only acceptable form of meditation for Christians, meditating on the Scriptures. How things have changed! Now many churches openly embrace and encourage a variety of methods of meditation, because they now recognize it as a spiritual practice that helps people achieve serenity and inner peace.

If you don't already meditate, you may want to start by using a passage of Scripture that is particularly meaningful to you. I always like to recommend portions of Psalm 139, which is appropriate for both Christians and Jews. (For this exercise, you may want to ignore verses 19–22, which are full of images of

Peace is our gift to each other.

—ELIE WIESEL

bloodshed—not good for your peace of mind!). Begin by meditating on small chunks, such as verses 1–6 or the last two verses.

If you already practice meditation, you may want to try something new, such as meditating using religious art as a focal point. A peaceful image can help clear out the clutter in our minds so we can settle into a meditative state more easily.

22

Freedom's Fascinating Power

None who have always been free can understand the
terrible, fascinating power of the hope of freedom to
those who are not free.

—**Pearl S. Buck**

"The terrible, fascinating power of the hope of freedom."
That's the energy that drives people to risk everything for the
sake of freedom. In my own lifetime, I've witnessed several
inspiring examples of extraordinary people who gambled on
freedom and won in a big way: Lech Walesa in Poland, Nelson
Mandela and Desmond Tutu in South Africa, Václav Havel in
Czechoslovakia, and Martin Luther King Jr. in the United
States. Without hope, they never could have accomplished
what they did; their drive would have disappeared long before
they came close to reaching their goal.

Havel, a playwright and essayist, is something of a personal
hero of mine, having written these words: "A writer can only
remain honest if he keeps free of party labels." That was long
before label-free writers learned to use gender-free pronouns,
but that's not the point. Let's assume that today he would
include me in that sentence; the point is that in his quest for
freedom, he never turned a blind eye to the abuses on the part

of liberals, who appeared to be fighting for the same things he was. His commitment to truth and to personal integrity has gotten him into more than one vat of hot water with both his political and financial backers.

His outspokenness may have lost him a lot of support over the years, but he never lost hope that if he and other Czechs—writers, workers, merchants, people from all walks of life—would keep exerting pressure on the then-communist government, they would see the reforms they were fighting for. In the end, his loss of support was meaningless; in 1993, he was elected the first president of the new Czech Republic. As president, he has said things that you're fairly sure no other head of state has ever said, crediting Lou Reed of the Velvet Underground with getting him elected, citing the power to get his plays performed to his liking as one of the best things about being president, and looking forward with relief to the end of his term so he could stop having to be so diplomatic.

But back to hope, which Havel—who was imprisoned for nearly five years for criticizing the government—believes is closely linked to the very meaning of life:

> Often people confuse hope with prognostics. Prognostics is the science of studying whatever happens around you in the world. With it either you will make a positive prognosis (because you are an optimist) or a negative prognosis (which would have a pessimistic impact on the people around you). But it is very important to differentiate. Hope is not

Losing hope is like losing your freedom, losing yourself.

—REBBE NACHMAN OF BRESLOV

127

prognosis. Hope is something that I see as the state of the spirit. If life had no sense, then there would be no hope, because the very sense of life, the meaning of life, is closely linked with hope.[20]

The classic Christian text on hope, one that describes the way faith impacts the "state of the spirit," is found in Hebrews 11:1: "Now faith is the assurance of things hoped for, the conviction of things not seen" (NRSV). This verse has provided an ongoing source of hope to people who have lost their freedom or have never known what living in freedom is like. So has the rest of the chapter, which gives an account of what has come to be called the hall of fame of faith—the stories of Abel, Enoch, Abraham, Sarah, Isaac, Jacob, Joseph, Moses, and Rahab. And then the writer seems to get frustrated; there's just not enough time to tell about others such as Gideon, Barak, Samson, Jephthah, David, Samuel, and the prophets.

For people who live in oppressive circumstances, the clincher is found in verse 13: "All these people died having faith. They didn't receive the things that God had promised them, but they saw these things coming in the distant future and rejoiced. They acknowledged that they were living as strangers with no permanent home on earth" (God's Word). That's the sense you get when reading about people who struggle for freedom in tyrannical, repressive regimes; they have hope for a better future but not necessarily in their lifetime; they have hope on Earth for future generations, but hope for themselves is only to be found in the afterlife. (The fall of the Soviet Union was not

If you assume that there's no hope, you guarantee that there will be no hope. If you assume that there is an instinct for freedom, there are opportunities to change things, there's a chance for you to contribute to making a better world.

—NOAM CHOMSKY

something that many Russians had any hope of seeing before they died; events moved so swiftly toward the end that it took a while for people to grasp the reality that their government had actually collapsed.)

Unlike Martin Luther King Jr. and so many others, Havel is among the fortunate few who have had the privilege of enjoying the fruit of their freedom-fighting labor. "Enjoy," of course, is a figurative term; you get the distinct impression that he and the others who emerged victorious in their own lifetimes will never be content and will never stop fighting for as long as they live—even though much of the oppression will outlast them. They will die, but their hope will not.

REFLECTION

Outside of India, not many people know the name Rabindranath Tagore, although his poetry is gradually gaining wider recognition in the United States. In 1913, he became the first non-European to be awarded the Nobel Prize for Literature; his literary output is nothing short of astonishing. He also wrote several thousand songs, one of which became India's national anthem. Like Václav Havel, he was a writer turned political activist and freedom fighter. So significant was his work that Jawaharlal Nehru, India's first prime minister and the father of Indira Gandhi, compared him to Mahatma Gandhi, and *Time* magazine's Asia edition named him one of the one hundred most influential Asians of the twentieth century.

Most of the important things in the world have been accomplished by people who have kept on trying when there seemed to be no hope at all.

—DALE CARNEGIE

Wait, Israel, for God. Wait with hope. Hope now; hope always!

—PSALM 131:3
(*THE MESSAGE*)

In this prayer, he expresses the heart of hope—that its power lies not in a particular outcome but in its capacity to overcome fear in the midst of struggle:

> Let me not pray to be sheltered from dangers but to be fearless in facing them.... Let me not crave in anxious fear to be saved but hope for the patience to win my freedom. Grant me that I may not be a coward, feeling your mercy in my success alone; but let me find the grasp of your hand in my failure.[21]

In what areas of your life do you need to experience true freedom? What dangers—what obstacles—lie between you and the freedom you crave? Do you feel God's mercy only when you enjoy success—or have you been able to find the grasp of God's hand even in your failures?

PRACTICE

Give yourself the gift of spiritual freedom. Go and do something wild and crazy in your worship of God, if that's not your typical nature. Or try something calm and serene if it is. I've been both a wild and crazy charismatic and a calm and serene quasi-contemplative, plus all things in between. Once I left a fairly rigid faith community, I began to revel in the varieties of faith expressions out there. Each one has enriched my life in some way. We need to remember that the freedom God gives applies to all of life, including our means of worship.

I find hope in the darkest of days, and focus in the brightest. I do not judge the universe.

—**DALAI LAMA**

If you lose hope, somehow you lose the vitality that keeps life moving, you lose that courage to be, that quality that helps you go on in spite of it all.

—**MARTIN LUTHER KING JR.**

The Worst That Could Happen

However deceitful hope may be, yet she carries us on
pleasantly to the end of life.

—François de La Rochefoucauld

So here we are, almost at the end of our journey through
the different ways of looking at hope, the varieties of benefits
hope has to offer, the evidence that hope is much more solid
than are the wispy, ephemeral concepts we associate it with.
Still not convinced? Then this chapter is for you, the holdout
on hope.

A seventeenth-century nobleman and "man of letters,"
François de La Rochefoucauld hears you, even today. The man
speaks your language. "However deceitful hope may be" is the
thought with which he begins one of his celebrated maxims.
Hope is a deceitful thing, at least sometimes. It makes us think
that the most outlandish things can actually happen. It teases us
into believing that people can change, cars are dependable, and
money will last—and then it taunts us with the reality that people resist change, cars break down, and money runs out.
Deceitful little urchin, that hope.

But wait. Our man of letters continues his thought: " ... yet she carries us on pleasantly to the end of life." Aha! Gotcha! After lulling you into believing he's in your corner, he pulls a one-eighty on you and turns this thinking around completely. Now who's the deceitful one?

Hope, it seems, is a vehicle, and a female one at that. (Okay, forget the female part; we've long stopped attaching gender-specific pronouns to nouns, haven't we? If it weren't for those pesky ships ...) Hope "carries us." I think we could end his thought there quite nicely. Hope does indeed carry us. It carries us through tragedy, turmoil, sorrow, boredom, fear, illness, delay, horror, and so much more. But let's let the duke finish his thought.

Hope "carries us on pleasantly to the end of life." As fickle as hope is—fulfilling your dreams at one turn, quashing them at another—it still proves itself to be the better means to get us through our life on Earth. Granted, the other means, despair, may actually have proven to be more trustworthy in your own life; if you've ever wallowed in despair, you know how completely you can trust it to produce more despair, and then even more. But which is the pleasanter means to the end? I think the voice from the seventeenth century has got you there.

The skeptic in you is now afraid. What if La Rochefoucauld is right? Where does that leave you? It leaves you with a lot to lose—a lot of negative thinking, for one thing, as well as your reputation as a cynic. And you stand to lose the certainty that has served you so well. You've always been certain that things

In all things it is better to hope than to despair.

—JOHANN WOLFGANG VON GOETHE

can only get worse, and what do you know? They do! Worst of all, you could lose face. What if you express the hope that you get the promotion you genuinely deserve, and some upstart grabs it right out of your deserving hands? Won't you lose face? Maybe, maybe not. It depends a lot on your attitude in the face of disappointment; go back to chapter 2 for a refresher.

If you're a true dyed-in-the-wool cynic, one who has little hope in humanity or the future, you may make for a popular dinner guest—what fun is a dinner party without a little provocation?—or a talented newspaper columnist or Sunday morning television commentator, but the path you've chosen is by far the less pleasant one. This is it, your one and only life. You can choose to make the way of despair the course for your life, or you can choose the way of hope. They'll both take you to the same end, but what's the worst that could happen if you choose the way of hope for your one and only life? Maybe your last regret will be that you hadn't been more cynical and despairing, but somehow I doubt it.

Of course, anyone who has gotten to this chapter is not truly cynical or skeptical, and I hope not despairing. But it's important for all of us to be aware of the fallacies of hopeless thinking, because we will know people throughout our lives who are, to put it bluntly, downers. They can subtly pull us in to their negative way of thinking if we're not careful to remember how pointless it is to choose the way of despair. I'm acutely aware of the power of infectious negativity, and I may think I'm immune to it at this point in my life, but it comes in such a subtle package that it can take a while before you realize you've opened yourself up to its influence.

You'll never regret choosing hope. Never. It *does* carry us on pleasantly to the end of life. I'm past caring what others think of the optimism I have for the future—my future as well as the future of humanity. What's the worst that could happen? I have no idea. I've stopped thinking the worst.

REFLECTION

What do you think the payoffs of cynicism are? There must be a payoff; people live the way they do because there's some benefit in living that way. In my days as a cynic, I think the payoff was twofold: I loved being right, and cynics can always make things that go right appear as if they've gone wrong, and I secretly enjoyed provoking people. Think of the cynics you know; what have they gained from being negative?

Maybe they have a taste for vermin. Look at this wonderful image from nineteenth-century preacher Henry Ward Beecher:

> The cynic is one who never sees a good quality in a man, and never fails to see a bad one. He is the human owl, vigilant in darkness and blind to light, mousing for vermin, and never seeing noble game.

I find great amusement in that image. But here's a serious question: how can "human owls" be transformed into people of hope?

It's a lot better to hope than not to.

—BENJAMIN J. STEIN

PRACTICE

Brother Lawrence was a seventeenth-century Carmelite lay brother who would likely be dumbfounded if he could see the impact his life has had on subsequent generations. Although in his later years he rarely ventured beyond the grounds of his monastery, his life became known to the world through the eyes of one frequent visitor, a Catholic cleric who befriended Lawrence and later published his memories of his friend and excerpts from the letters they exchanged. The published book was titled *The Practice of the Presence of God*, and it remains a classic in the literature of faith and spirituality.[22]

Brother Lawrence's way of thinking and living provides a perfect antidote to cynicism. Everything he did was saturated in the love of God and the love he had for God. His work became a sacrament. Though he had a "great aversion" to kitchen work, he spent fifteen years working in the monastery's kitchen and found the work to be both easy and pleasant. It is not the greatness of work that matters, he believed, but the love with which it is performed.

Prayer was his way of life. While others hustled and bustled about the kitchen, Brother Lawrence proceeded at a meditative pace—not slowly but calmly, working just as efficiently as the others if not more so. Nothing disturbed his tranquility or composure, not even when several people would be calling out to him at the same time as he worked.

"In continuing the practice of conversing with God throughout each day, and quickly seeking His forgiveness when I fell or

> The road that is built in hope is more pleasant to the traveler than the road built in despair, even though they both lead to the same destination.
>
> —MARIAN ZIMMER BRADLEY

135

strayed, His presence has become as easy and natural to me now as it once was difficult to attain," Lawrence wrote.

Practice the presence of God in your life. Saturate your life with an awareness of God's love; see your work, no matter what it is, as a sacrament, an act of grace. That's the way of hope.

All things are possible to him who believes, yet more to him who hopes, more still to him who loves, and most of all to him who practices and perseveres in these three virtues.

—BROTHER LAWRENCE

24

A Better Life to Come

Not only is another world possible, she is on her way. On a quiet day, I can hear her breathing.

—Arundhati Roy

Can you hear the breathing of another world—the soft, rhythmic whisper of the life to come? On a quiet afternoon, sitting in the presence of a dying hospice patient, I often feel a ripple of something wafting through the room. Call it God, call it angels, call it what you will, it's there, and its breath holds the promise of a better life to come.

People whose loved ones have experienced hospice care likely know what I mean. Because the emphasis is on "dying well," patients under hospice care are allowed to die at home on their own terms. And when that happens—when patients are permitted to go gently into that good night—the separation between this world and the next becomes nearly indistinguishable.

Celtic Christians also would have understood what I mean. They believed that certain geographical areas were "thin places"—places identified as holy ground, places where the line between heaven and earth was uncommonly thin, places where those with spiritual sight could see the heavenly realm beyond.

To me, there is no more holy ground on Earth than at the bedside of someone who is dying well. That person's last hours in the earthly realm become thin moments, a time when the veil between heaven and earth is lifted. We can only sit on the sidelines and imagine the unseen drama that is unfolding; the patient is the one who gets the benefit of a clear view. For the first time in a long time, the patient has the advantage over the healthy.

William Lawson, a Boston pastor, knew about thin moments. To my knowledge, he never used that term. But the following story, which he apparently never had published, shows his profound understanding of that unveiled sacred moment when we leave the safety and security of the only life we've ever known and awaken to the reality of another world:

> Two unborn twins floated snug and secure in their mother's womb. But they faced an uncertain future, an uncertain passage to a new life. Weeks passed into months, and with the advent of each new month, the twins noticed a change in each other, and each twin began to see change in himself.
>
> "We are changing," said the one to the other. "What can it mean?"
>
> "It means," said the other, "that we are drawing near to birth."
>
> "Were it up to me, I would live here forever!" the first twin said.

Listen now to the gentle whispers of hope.

—CHARLES D. BRODHEAD

"But we must be born," said the other. "It has happened to all the others who were here before." For indeed there was evidence of life-there-before, as the mother had borne other children. "But is there life after birth?"

"How can there be life after birth?" cried the first twin. "Do we not shed our life cord? And have you ever talked to one that has been born? Has anyone ever re-entered the womb after birth? No!" The first fell into despair, and in his despair he moaned, "If the purpose of conception and all our growth is that it be ended in birth, then truly our life is absurd." Resigned to despair, he stabbed the darkness with his unseeing eyes, and as he clutched his precious life cord to his chest, he said, "If this is so, and life is absurd, then there really can be no mother."

"But there is a mother," protested the other. "Who else gave us nourishment and our world?"

"We get our own nourishment, and our world has always been here," replied the first twin. "And if there is a mother, where is she? Have you ever seen her? Does she ever talk to you? No! We invented the mother because it satisfied a need in us. It made us feel secure and happy."

Thus while one raved and despaired, the other resigned himself to birth and placed his trust in the hands of his unseen Mother. Hours stretched into days, and days became weeks, and then the time came. Both knew their birth was at hand, and both feared what they did not know. They cried as they were born into the light—and they coughed as they gasped the dry air. And when they were sure they had been born, they opened their eyes, seeing for the first time!

They found themselves cradled in the warm love of their Mother's arms. They lay open-mouthed, awestruck before an overwhelming beauty and truth that was far more wonderful than anything they could ever have hoped for.[23]

I hope that when my time comes God will grant me the opportunity to die well. But even if I die under traumatic circumstances, surrounded by medical personnel whose heroic efforts to save my life keep me isolated from the people who mean the most to me, I won't care one bit that I did not die a peaceful death in the warmth and comfort of my own home. The moment I am birthed into that other world, that better life, I believe God will cradle me safely and securely, just as a loving mother cradles her newborn. I will discover that trusting in the hands of my unseen Mother was no futile act of wishful thinking, nor was God merely an invention that satisfied a need in me.

Listen carefully for the breathing of another world. It may come as little more than a faint whisper, but it speaks of the infinite invisible realities of the better life that awaits us. When we grasp the concept that death is another birth, we can hear that whisper far more distinctly. Hold on to the hope embraced in that whisper. Another world is on its way.

Reflection

What does the afterlife look like to you? If you are a Christian, what do you think of the description of heaven in the book of Revelation? Are you afraid to die? Are you looking forward to the afterlife? If so, why? If not, why not? If your faith tradition offers a different perspective on death, how does that affect your attitude to life? Are you looking forward to something beyond the ending of an individual life? It's okay to think about these things; it doesn't indicate that you have a morbid fascination with death.

Practice

The practice of keeping vigil is one that crosses all religious lines. Though frequently associated with death—as in praying at the bedside of a dying person—vigils are also associated with spiritual battle and spiritual hope. By staying up or arising during the night and spending time in prayer, we both oppose the darkness and await the dawn.

There's something about the stillness and the darkness of night that intensifies your awareness of God. Spending time with God when everyone else is asleep, in a quiet and

I cannot conceive that God could make such a species as the human merely to live and die on this earth. If I did not believe in a future state, I should believe in no God.

—John Adams

undistracted atmosphere, carries with it the idea of standing guard while others rest. There's an indescribable sense of responsibility and even honor that accompanies keeping vigil; you feel honored that God has entrusted you with that responsibility. It doesn't matter whether you stay up all night or wake up during the night for a few minutes of prayer; whatever time you devote to keeping vigil is time well spent.

Those who hope in the Lord will renew their strength. They will soar on wings like eagles; they will run and not grow weary, they will walk and not be faint.

—Isaiah 40:31 (NIV)

Ending with Hope

I'm sure you know the saying "Watch what you ask for, because you just might get it." The idea is that the things we ask for may cause us more grief than we bargained for. A similar principle applies to writers: Watch what you write about, because you just might get a chance to question what you've written.

More than one person reminded me of that principle as I was writing *The Sacred Art of Forgiveness: Forgiving Ourselves and Others through God's Grace* (SkyLight Paths Publishing). Some were writers; they knew what it was like to write about faith and pretty near lose it in the process. One was a pastor's wife; presumably, ministers need to watch what they preach, which may be why some are so reluctant to preach against temptation. But nothing happened. No one offended me. No one hurt me. No one took the parking spot that they could clearly see I had been waiting for in the hot Florida sun for *minutes*. I had nothing new to forgive, and I committed no major blunders that I needed to seek forgiveness for.

Not so, however, with *Finding Hope*. Within days of signing the book contract, our house caught fire. While we were living in a hotel during the fire restoration, we got hit with an unrelated and, for us, exorbitant IRS bill. After we moved back into the house—and long before the restoration was complete—I was bedridden for weeks with a mysterious and unrelenting muscle spasm. Not only was I in pain that no medication could relieve, I was also unable to work. At the same time, a close relative in crisis suddenly became despondent and suicidal.

There were moments when I could have sworn that the fire restoration crew had taken my last shred of hope, boxed it up, and put it in storage with the rest of our personal property. The final scenes of *Indiana Jones and the Raiders of the Lost Ark* frequently came to mind; finding hope was like trying to find the lost ark in a numbered carton amid thousands of others in a vast government warehouse.

Or so it seemed.

I won't deny that for several months I had a hard time believing our lives would ever get back to a state that remotely resembled normal. And although those were months of intense and at times debilitating stress, I can look back on that time today with an unexplainable detachment. That's another aspect of the power of hope—it gives us the resilience to recover from setbacks and begin to look forward to the future once again, on occasion with remarkable speed.

The irony is that some factors that produced so much stress haven't actually changed. The intensity of the situation has lessened, and the person in crisis has received some much-needed help before any real damage was done. But we're at a standstill with regard to the house, we're still in debt to the IRS, and the muscle spasm is an indication of a much more serious disorder. And yet, my hope has been restored. I never lost it completely; I knew it was still around somewhere, but there were moments when it seemed to have evaporated.

If you were to ask me today what makes me so hopeful about a largely unchanged situation, I'm not sure I could give you an answer that would satisfy you. I'm sure that someday we'll have the IRS off our backs, we'll get the house back together again, and I'll be able to make the necessary adjustments to my life to accommodate this new health challenge. My hope, though, does not rest in those outcomes. My hope just *is*. It's a fact of my life just as real as my age or the color of my eyes. It's a part of me. As much a part of me as the air I breathe.

Since I started out this discussion of hope with the words of Gerald May, it's fitting that I should close with his words as well:

So in the end I am left only with hope. I hope the nights really are transformative. I hope every dawn brings deeper love, for each of us individually and for the world as a whole. I hope that John of the Cross was right when he said the intellect is transformed into faith, and the will into love, and the memory into ... hope.[24]

In the end, we are all left only with hope. But that's a good thing, because *la esperanza muere al último.* Hope dies last.

Acknowledgments

Thank you to:

- Maura Shaw, for once again suggesting a book that afforded me an opportunity to write from my heart, and the rest of the staff at SkyLight Paths and Jewish Lights.

- Andrea Jaeger, for kindly agreeing to write the foreword and for providing an inspiring example of hope through her service to terminally ill children and their families. You can read about her organization at www.littlestar.org.

- Nancy Guthrie, for graciously allowing me to tell her story in chapter 12. More of her story, as well as photos of Hope and Gabriel, can be found at www.nancyguthrie.com.

- Alice, Eileen, Elaine, the other Elaine, Peggy, and Rae. I wish we could all get together in one place so those of you who don't know each other could discover the priceless treasure all of you are. Thank you for the prayers, the encouragement, the support, and especially the laughter.

- My sister, Merta Platt, and my brothers, Thurman Edwards and Bill DuPriest, for keeping me from losing every one of my marbles as I faced one challenge after another in the early part of 2006.

- John, Elizabeth, and Sarah, for their love and their support despite my increasingly intrusive and annoying writing habit. Maybe I'll get it all under control someday.

Credits

Scripture marked God's Word is taken from God's Word, copyright 1995 by God's Word to the Nations. Quotations are used by permission. All rights reserved.

Scripture marked NAS is taken from the New American Standard Bible, copyright 1960, 1962, 1963, 1968, 1971, 1972, 1973, 1975, 1977, 1995 by The Lockman Foundation. Used by permission.

Scripture marked NCV is taken from the New Century Version, copyright 1987, 1988, 1991 by Word Publishing, a division of Thomas Nelson, Inc. All rights reserved. Used by permission.

Scripture marked NIV is taken from the Holy Bible, New International Version. Copyright 1973, 1978, 1984 by International Bible Society. Used by permission of Zondervan Publishing House. All rights reserved.

Scripture marked NKJV is taken from the New King James Version, copyright 1982 by Thomas Nelson, Inc. All rights reserved. Used by permission.

Scripture marked NLT is taken from the Holy Bible, New Living Translation, copyright 1996. Used by permission of Tyndale House Publishers. All rights reserved.

Notes

1. Gerald May, *The Dark Night of the Soul: A Psychiatrist Explores the Connection between Darkness and Spiritual Growth* (San Francisco: HarperSanFrancisco, 2003), 192.
2. May, *The Dark Night of the Soul,* 193.
3. Gerald Mann, *When One Day at a Time Is Too Long: Hopeful Answers to Hard Questions* (Austin, TX: Riverbend Press, 1994), 289–90.
4. Sermon delivered October 23, 2005, at First United Methodist Church of Germantown, Philadelphia, PA. Posted at http://www.bethstroud.info/sermon20051023.shtml.
5. *The One Year Book of Personal Prayer: Inspirational Prayers and Thoughts for Each Day of the Year,* ed. Daniel Partner (Wheaton, IL: Tyndale House, 1991), May 10.
6. Depending on the source, this quote is attributed to either Charles Caleb Colton or the annoyingly prolific but wise Anonymous. Since Anonymous has not stepped forward to claim this quote as his or her own, I am crediting it to Colton, who at least has a complete name.
7. The Michael J. Fox Foundation for Parkinson's Research, http://www.michaeljfox.org.
8. Mann, *When One Day at a Time Is Too Long,* 38–39.
9. Mother Teresa of Calcutta, *A Gift for God: Prayers and Meditations* (New York: Harper & Row, 1975), p. 21.
10. The entire text of John's work, if you're interested, is posted at www.ccel.org/ccel/john_cross/dark_night.html; the site—the Christian Classics Ethereal Library, sponsored by Calvin College in Grand Rapids, Michigan—offers a wealth of documents, resources, and full-length books.
11. See http://www.salsa.net/peace/conv for information on the course, developed by peace activist Colman McCarthy and sponsored by the San Antonio PeaceCENTER.
12. Eugene Robinson, "Nation of Fear," *Washington Post,* May 16, 2006. Posted at http://www.washingtonpost.com/wp-dyn/content/article/2006/05/15/AR2006051501187_pf.html.
13. Jerome Groopman, *The Anatomy of Hope: How Patients Prevail in the Face of Illness* (New York: Random House, 2004), 255.

14. Groopman, *The Anatomy of Hope,* xvi.
15. William Styron, *Darkness Visible: A Memoir of Madness* (New York: Vintage Books, 1985), 62.
16. John Eldredge and Brent Curtis, *The Sacred Romance: Drawing Closer to the Heart of God* (Nashville: Thomas Nelson, 1997), 137. Brent Curtis, John Eldredge's best friend and coauthor, was killed in a hiking accident while on a retreat with John just as this book was released. I quote Eldredge more extensively because I have heard him speak on the Sacred Romance on many occasions.
17. John Eldredge, *The Journey of Desire: Searching for the Life We've Only Dreamed Of* (Nashville: Thomas Nelson, 2000), p. 3.
18. Ronald Boyd-MacMillan, *Faith That Endures: The Essential Guide to the Persecuted Church* (Grand Rapids, MI: Revell, 2006), 64.
19. Peace Pilgrim, "The Way of Peace," in *Peace Pilgrim: Her Life and Work in Her Own Words.* Posted at http://www.peacepilgrim.org/book/chapt8.htm.
20. From an undated interview with Václav Havel on the website Speak Truth to Power. Posted at http://www.speaktruth.org/defend/profiles/profile_27.asp.
21. Rabindranath Tagore, *Fruit-Gathering* (New York: The Macmillan Company, 1916). Posted on www.sacred-texts.com.
22. A printer-friendly copy of *The Practice of the Presence of God* can be found at www.practicegodspresence.com; it's about twenty pages. Another version of the book is posted on the Christian Classics Ethereal Library at www.ccel.org/ccel/lawrence/practice.html. And it's still available in print as well, after all these centuries; now *that's* a bestseller.
23. From a serman delivered by the Rev. Beth Appel at Calvary Presbyterian Church, San Francisco, on May 10, 1996, with story credited to the Rev. William Lawson. Posted at http://calvarypresbyterian.org/sermons/sermon.php?SermonID-87.
24. May, *The Dark Night of the Soul,* 191.

Suggestions for Further Reading on Hope

Boyd-MacMillan, Ronald. *Faith That Endures: The Essential Guide to the Persecuted Church.* Grand Rapids, MI: Revell, 2006.

Curtis, Brent, and John Eldredge. *The Sacred Romance: Drawing Closer to the Heart of God.* Nashville, TN: Thomas Nelson, 1997.

Ford, Marcia. *The Sacred Art of Forgiveness: Forgiving Ourselves and Others through God's Grace.* Woodstock, VT: SkyLight Paths Publishing, 2006.

Groopman, Jerome. *The Anatomy of Hope: How Patients Prevail in the Face of Illness.* New York: Random House, 2004.

Guthrie, Nancy. *Holding On to Hope: A Pathway through Suffering to the Heart of God.* Wheaton, IL: Tyndale House, 2002.

Lamm, Maurice. *The Power of Hope: The One Essential of Life and Love.* New York: Rawson Associates, 1995.

Mann, Gerald. *When One Day at a Time Is Too Long: Hopeful Answers to Hard Questions.* Austin, TX: Riverbend Press, 1994.

May, Gerald. *The Dark Night of the Soul: A Psychiatrist Explores the Connection between Darkness and Spiritual Growth.* San Francisco: HarperSanFrancisco, 2003.

Nachman of Breslov. *The Empty Chair: Finding Hope and Joy.* Woodstock, VT: Jewish Lights, 1994.

The One Year Book of Personal Prayer: Inspirational Prayers and Thoughts for Each Day of the Year. Edited by Daniel Partner. Wheaton, IL: Tyndale House, 1991.

Veninga, Robert. *A Gift of Hope: How We Survive Our Tragedies.* Boston: G.K. Hall, 1985.

Williamson, Marianne. *Everyday Grace: Having Hope, Finding Forgiveness, and Making Miracles.* New York: Riverhead Books, 2002.

Global Spiritual Perspectives

Spiritual Perspectives on America's Role as Superpower
by the Editors at SkyLight Paths

Are we the world's good neighbor or a global bully? From a spiritual perspective, what are America's responsibilities as the only remaining superpower? Contributors:

Dr. Beatrice Bruteau • Dr. Joan Brown Campbell •Tony Campolo • Rev. Forrest Church • Lama Surya Das • Matthew Fox • Kabir Helminski • Thich Nhat Hanh • Eboo Patel • Abbot M. Basil Pennington, ocso • Dennis Prager • Rosemary Radford Ruether • Wayne Teasdale • Rev. William McD. Tully • Rabbi Arthur Waskow • John Wilson

5½ x 8½, 256 pp, Quality PB, 978-1-893361-81-2 **$16.95**

Spiritual Perspectives on Globalization, 2nd Edition
Making Sense of Economic and Cultural Upheaval
by Ira Rifkin; Foreword by Dr. David Little, Harvard Divinity School

What is globalization? Surveys the religious landscape. Includes a new Discussion Guide designed for group use.

5½ x 8½, 256 pp, Quality PB, 978-1-59473-045-0 **$16.99**

Hinduism / Vedanta

The Four Yogas: A Guide to the Spiritual Paths of Action, Devotion, Meditation and Knowledge
by Swami Adiswarananda 6 x 9, 320 pp, HC, 978-1-59473-143-3 **$29.99**

Meditation & Its Practices: A Definitive Guide to Techniques and Traditions of Meditation in Yoga and Vedanta
by Swami Adiswarananda 6 x 9, 504 pp, Quality PB, 978-1-59473-105-1 **$19.99**

The Spiritual Quest and the Way of Yoga: The Goal, the Journey and the Milestones
by Swami Adiswarananda 6 x 9, 288 pp, HC, 978-1-59473-113-6 **$29.99**

Sri Ramakrishna, the Face of Silence
by Swami Nikhilananda and Dhan Gopal Mukerji; Edited with an Introduction by Swami Adiswarananda; Foreword by Dhan Gopal Mukerji II
Classic biographies present the life and thought of Sri Ramakrishna.
6 x 9, 352 pp, HC, 978-1-59473-115-0 **$29.99**

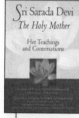

Sri Sarada Devi, The Holy Mother: Her Teachings and Conversations
Translated with Notes by Swami Nikhilananda; Edited with an Introduction by Swami Adiswarananda
6 x 9, 288 pp, HC, 978-1-59473-070-2 **$29.99**

The Vedanta Way to Peace and Happiness *by Swami Adiswarananda*
6 x 9, 240 pp, HC, 978-1-59473-034-4 **$29.99**

Vivekananda, World Teacher: His Teachings on the Spiritual Unity of Humankind
Edited and with an Introduction by Swami Adiswarananda
6 x 9, 272 pp, Quality PB, 978-1-59473-210-2 **$21.99**

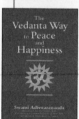

Sikhism

The First Sikh Spiritual Master
Timeless Wisdom from the Life and Teachings of Guru Nanak *by Harish Dhillon*
Tells the story of a unique spiritual leader who showed a gentle, peaceful path to God-realization while highlighting Guru Nanak's quest for tolerance and compassion. 6 x 9, 192 pp, Quality PB, 978-1-59473-209-6 **$16.99**

Or phone, fax, mail or e-mail to: SKYLIGHT PATHS Publishing
Sunset Farm Offices, Route 4 • P.O. Box 237 • Woodstock, Vermont 05091
Tel: (802) 457-4000 • Fax: (802) 457-4004 • www.skylightpaths.com
Credit card orders: (800) 962-4544 (8:30AM–5:30PM ET Monday–Friday)
Generous discounts on quantity orders. SATISFACTION GUARANTEED. Prices subject to change.

Midrash Fiction / Folktales

Abraham's Bind & Other Bible Tales of Trickery, Folly, Mercy and Love
by Michael J. Caduto
New retellings of episodes in the lives of familiar biblical characters explore relevant life lessons.
6 x 9, 224 pp, HC, 978-1-59473-186-0 **$19.99**

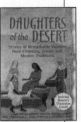

Daughters of the Desert: Stories of Remarkable Women from Christian, Jewish and Muslim Traditions
by Claire Rudolf Murphy, Meghan Nuttall Sayres, Mary Cronk Farrell, Sarah Conover and Betsy Wharton
Breathes new life into the old tales of our female ancestors in faith. Uses traditional scriptural passages as starting points, then with vivid detail fills in historical context and place. Chapters reveal the voices of Sarah, Hagar, Huldah, Esther, Salome, Mary Magdalene, Lydia, Khadija, Fatima and many more. Historical fiction ideal for readers of all ages. Quality paperback includes reader's discussion guide.
5½ x 8½, 192 pp, Quality PB, 978-1-59473-106-8 **$14.99**
HC, 192 pp, 978-1-893361-72-0 **$19.95**

The Triumph of Eve & Other Subversive Bible Tales
by Matt Biers-Ariel
Many people were taught and remember only a one-dimensional Bible. These engaging retellings are the antidote to this—they're witty, often hilarious, always profound, and invite you to grapple with questions and issues that are often hidden in the original text.
5½ x 8½, 192 pp, HC, 978-1-59473-040-5 **$19.99**

Also avail.: The Triumph of Eve Teacher's Guide
8½ x 11, 44 pp, PB, 978-1-59473-152-5 **$8.99**

Wisdom in the Telling
Finding Inspiration and Grace in Traditional Folktales and Myths Retold
by Lorraine Hartin-Gelardi
6 x 9, 224 pp, HC, 978-1-59473-185-3 **$19.99**

Religious Etiquette / Reference

How to Be a Perfect Stranger, 4th Edition: The Essential Religious Etiquette Handbook
Edited by Stuart M. Matlins and Arthur J. Magida
The indispensable guidebook to help the well-meaning guest when visiting other people's religious ceremonies. A straightforward guide to the rituals and celebrations of the major religions and denominations in the United States and Canada from the perspective of an interested guest of any other faith, based on information obtained from authorities of each religion. Belongs in every living room, library and office.
Covers:
African American Methodist Churches • Assemblies of God • Bahá'í • Baptist • Buddhist • Christian Church (Disciples of Christ) • Christian Science (Church of Christ, Scientist) • Churches of Christ • Episcopalian and Anglican • Hindu • Islam • Jehovah's Witnesses • Jewish • Lutheran • Mennonite/Amish • Methodist • Mormon (Church of Jesus Christ of Latter-day Saints) • Native American/First Nations • Orthodox Churches • Pentecostal Church of God • Presbyterian • Quaker (Religious Society of Friends) • Reformed Church in America/Canada • Roman Catholic • Seventh-day Adventist • Sikh • Unitarian Universalist • United Church of Canada • United Church of Christ
6 x 9, 432 pp, Quality PB, 978-1-59473-140-2 **$19.99**

The Perfect Stranger's Guide to Funerals and Grieving Practices: A Guide to Etiquette in Other
People's Religious Ceremonies *Edited by Stuart M. Matlins*
6 x 9, 240 pp, Quality PB, 978-1-893361-20-1 **$16.95**

The Perfect Stranger's Guide to Wedding Ceremonies: A Guide to Etiquette in Other People's Religious
Ceremonies *Edited by Stuart M. Matlins*
6 x 9, 208 pp, Quality PB, 978-1-893361-19-5 **$16.95**

Children's Spirituality

Remembering My Grandparent: A Kid's Own Grief Workbook in the Christian Tradition
by Nechama Liss-Levinson, PhD, and Rev. Molly Phinney Baskette, MDiv
8 x 10, 48 pp, 2-color text, HC, 978-1-59473-212-6 **$16.99** *For ages 7–13*

Does God Ever Sleep? *by Joan Sauro, CSJ; Full-color photos*
A charming nighttime reminder that God is always present in our lives.
10 x 8½, 32 pp, Quality PB, Full-color photos, 978-1-59473-110-5 **$8.99** *For ages 3–6*

Does God Forgive Me? *by August Gold; Full-color photos by Diane Hardy Waller*
Gently shows how God forgives all that we do if we are truly sorry.
10 x 8½, 32 pp, Quality PB, Full-color photos, 978-1-59473-142-6 **$8.99** *For ages 3–6*

God Said Amen *by Sandy Eisenberg Sasso; Full-color illus. by Avi Katz*
A warm and inspiring tale of two kingdoms that shows us that we need only reach out to each other to find the answers to our prayers.
9 x 12, 32 pp, HC, Full-color illus., 978-1-58023-080-3 **$16.95** *For ages 4 & up (a Jewish Lights book)*

How Does God Listen? *by Kay Lindahl; Full-color photos by Cynthia Maloney*
How do we know when God is listening to us? Children will find the answers to these questions as they engage their senses while the story unfolds, learning how God listens in the wind, waves, clouds, hot chocolate, perfume, our tears and our laughter.
10 x 8½, 32 pp, Quality PB, Full-color photos, 978-1-59473-084-9 **$8.99** *For ages 3–6*

In God's Hands *by Lawrence Kushner and Gary Schmidt; Full-color illus. by Matthew J. Baeck*
9 x 12, 32 pp, Full-color illus., HC, 978-1-58023-224-1 **$16.99** *For ages 5 & up (a Jewish Lights book)*

In God's Name *by Sandy Eisenberg Sasso; Full-color illus. by Phoebe Stone*
Like an ancient myth in its poetic text and vibrant illustrations, this award-winning modern fable about the search for God's name celebrates the diversity and, at the same time, the unity of all the people of the world. 9 x 12, 32 pp, HC, Full-color illus., 978-1-879045-26-2 **$16.99** *For ages 4 & up (a Jewish Lights book)*

Also available in Spanish: El nombre de Dios 9 x 12, 32 pp, HC, Full-color illus., 978-1-893361-63-8 **$16.95**

In Our Image: God's First Creatures *by Nancy Sohn Swartz; Full-color illus. by Melanie Hall*
A playful new twist on the Genesis story—from the perspective of the animals. Celebrates the interconnectedness of nature and the harmony of all living things.
9 x 12, 32 pp, HC, Full-color illus., 978-1-879045-99-6 **$16.95** *For ages 4 & up (a Jewish Lights book)*

Noah's Wife: The Story of Naamah *by Sandy Eisenberg Sasso; Full-color illus. by Bethanne Andersen*
This new story, based on an ancient text, opens readers' religious imaginations to new ideas about the well-known story of the Flood. When God tells Noah to bring the animals of the world onto the ark, God also calls on Naamah, Noah's wife, to save each plant on Earth.
9 x 12, 32 pp, HC, Full-color illus., 978-1-58023-134-3 **$16.95** *For ages 4 & up (a Jewish Lights book)*

Also available: Naamah: Noah's Wife (A Board Book) *by Sandy Eisenberg Sasso; Full-color illus. by Bethanne Andersen*
5 x 5, 24 pp, Board Book, Full-color illus., 978-1-893361-56-0 **$7.99** *For ages 0–4*

Where Does God Live? *by August Gold and Matthew J. Perlman*
Using simple, everyday examples that children can relate to, this colorful book helps young readers develop a personal understanding of God.
10 x 8½, 32 pp, Quality PB, Full-color photo illus., 978-1-893361-39-3 **$8.99** *For ages 3–6*

Children's Spirituality—Board Books

Adam and Eve's New Day (A Board Book)
by Sandy Eisenberg Sasso; Full-color illus. by Joani Keller Rothenberg
A lesson in hope for every child who has worried about what comes next. Abridged from *Adam and Eve's First Sunset*. 5 x 5, 24 pp, Full-color illus., Board Book, 978-1-59473-205-8 **$7.99** *For ages 0–4*

How Did the Animals Help God? (A Board Book)
by Nancy Sohn Swartz; Full-color illus. by Melanie Hall
Abridged from *In Our Image*, God asks all of nature to offer gifts to humankind—with a promise that they will care for creation in return. 5 x 5, 24 pp, Board Book, Full-color illus., 978-1-59473-044-3 **$7.99** *For ages 0–4*

Where Is God? (A Board Book)
by Lawrence and Karen Kushner; Full-color illus. by Dawn W. Majewski
A gentle way for young children to explore how God is with us every day, in every way. Abridged from *Because Nothing Looks Like God*. 5 x 5, 24 pp, Board Book, Full-color illus., 978-1-893361-17-1 **$7.99** *For ages 0–4*

What Does God Look Like? (A Board Book)
by Lawrence and Karen Kushner; Full-color illus. by Dawn W. Majewski
A simple way for young children to explore the ways that we "see" God. Abridged from *Because Nothing Looks Like God*. 5 x 5, 24 pp, Board Book, Full-color illus., 978-1-893361-23-2 **$7.95** *For ages 0–4*

How Does God Make Things Happen? (A Board Book)
by Lawrence and Karen Kushner; Full-color illus. by Dawn W. Majewski
A charming invitation for young children to explore how God makes things happen in our world. Abridged from *Because Nothing Looks Like God*. 5 x 5, 24 pp, Board Book, Full-color illus., 978-1-893361-24-9 **$7.95** *For ages 0–4*

What Is God's Name? (A Board Book)
by Sandy Eisenberg Sasso; Full-color illus. by Phoebe Stone
Everyone and everything in the world has a name. What is God's name? Abridged from the award-winning *In God's Name*. 5 x 5, 24 pp, Board Book, Full-color illus., 978-1-893361-10-2 **$7.99** *For ages 0–4*

What You Will See Inside ...

This important new series of books, each with many full-color photos, is designed to show children ages 6 and up the Who, What, When, Where, Why and How of traditional houses of worship, liturgical celebrations, and rituals of different world faiths, empowering them to respect and understand their own religious traditions—and those of their friends and neighbors.

What You Will See Inside a Catholic Church
by Reverend Michael Keane; Foreword by Robert J. Keeley, EdD; Full-color photos by Aaron Pepis
8½ x 10½, 32 pp, Full-color photos, HC, 978-1-893361-54-6 **$17.95**
Also available in Spanish: **Lo que se puede ver dentro de una iglesia católica**
8½ x 10½, 32 pp, Full-color photos, HC, 978-1-893361-66-9 **$16.95**

What You Will See Inside a Hindu Temple
by Dr. Mahendra Jani and Dr. Vandana Jani; Full-color photos by Neirah Bhargava and Vijay Dave
8½ x 10½, 32 pp, Full-color photos, HC, 978-1-59473-116-7 **$17.99**

What You Will See Inside a Mosque
by Aisha Karen Khan; Full-color photos by Aaron Pepis
8½ x 10½, 32 pp, Full-color photos, HC, 978-1-893361-60-7 **$16.95**

What You Will See Inside a Synagogue
by Rabbi Lawrence A. Hoffman and Dr. Ron Wolfson; Full-color photos by Bill Aron
8½ x 10½, 32 pp, Full-color photos, HC, 978-1-59473-012-2 **$17.99**

Sacred Texts—SkyLight Illuminations Series
Andrew Harvey, Series Editor

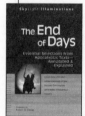

Offers today's spiritual seeker an accessible entry into the great classic texts of the world's spiritual traditions. Each classic is presented in an accessible translation, with facing pages of guided commentary from experts, giving you the keys you need to understand the history, context and meaning of the text. This series enables you, whatever your background, to experience and understand classic spiritual texts directly, and to make them a part of your life.

CHRISTIANITY

The End of Days: Essential Selections from Apocalyptic Texts—Annotated & Explained
Annotation by Robert G. Clouse
Introduces you to the beliefs and values held by those who rely on the promises found in the Book of Revelation.
5½ x 8½, 192 pp, Quality PB, 978-1-59473-170-9 **$16.99**

The Hidden Gospel of Matthew: Annotated & Explained
Translation & Annotation by Ron Miller
Takes you deep into the text cherished around the world to discover the words and events that have the strongest connection to the historical Jesus. 5½ x 8½, 272 pp, Quality PB, 978-1-59473-038-2 **$16.99**

The Lost Sayings of Jesus: Teachings from Ancient Christian, Jewish, Gnostic and Islamic Sources—Annotated & Explained
Translation & Annotation by Andrew Phillip Smith; Foreword by Stephan A. Hoeller
This collection of more than three hundred sayings depicts Jesus as a Wisdom teacher who speaks to people of all faiths as a mystic and spiritual master. 5½ x 8½, 240 pp, Quality PB, 978-1-59473-172-3 **$16.99**

Philokalia: The Eastern Christian Spiritual Texts—Selections Annotated & Explained
Annotation by Allyne Smith; Translation by G. E. H. Palmer, Phillip Sherrard and Bishop Kallistos Ware
The first approachable introduction to the wisdom of the Philokalia, which is the classic text of Eastern Christian spirituality. 5½ x 8½, 256 pp, Quality PB, 978-1-59473-103-7 **$16.99**

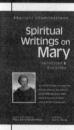

Spiritual Writings on Mary: Annotated & Explained
Annotation by Mary Ford-Grabowsky; Foreword by Andrew Harvey
Examines the role of Mary, the mother of Jesus, as a source of inspiration in history and in life today.
5½ x 8½, 288 pp, Quality PB, 978-1-59473-001-6 **$16.99**

The Way of a Pilgrim: Annotated & Explained
Translation & Annotation by Gleb Pokrovsky; Foreword by Andrew Harvey
This classic of Russian spirituality is the delightful account of one man who sets out to learn the prayer of the heart, also known as the "Jesus prayer." 5½ x 8½, 160 pp, Illus., Quality PB, 978-1-893361-31-7 **$14.95**

MORMONISM

The Book of Mormon: Selections Annotated & Explained
Annotation by Jana Riess; Foreword by Phyllis Tickle
Explores the sacred epic that is cherished by more than twelve million members of the LDS church as the keystone of their faith. 5½ x 8½ , 272 pp, Quality PB, 978-1-59473-076-4 **$16.99**

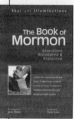

NATIVE AMERICAN

Native American Stories of the Sacred: Annotated & Explained
Retold & Annotated by Evan T. Pritchard
Intended for more than entertainment, these teaching tales contain elegantly simple illustrations of time-honored truths. 5½ x 8½, 272 pp, Quality PB, 978-1-59473-112-9 **$16.99**

Sacred Texts—cont.

GNOSTICISM

The Gospel of Philip: Annotated & Explained
Translation & Annotation by Andrew Phillip Smith; Foreword by Stevan Davies
Reveals otherwise unrecorded sayings of Jesus and fragments of Gnostic mythology.
5½ x 8½, 160 pp, Quality PB, 978-1-59473-111-2 **$16.99**

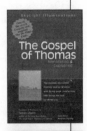

The Gospel of Thomas: Annotated & Explained
Translation & Annotation by Stevan Davies Sheds new light on the origins of Christianity and portrays Jesus as a wisdom-loving sage. 5½ x 8½, 192 pp, Quality PB, 978-1-893361-45-4 **$16.99**

The Secret Book of John: The Gnostic Gospel—Annotated & Explained
Translation & Annotation by Stevan Davies The most significant and influential text of the ancient Gnostic religion. 5½ x 8½, 208 pp, Quality PB, 978-1-59473-082-5 **$16.99**

JUDAISM

The Divine Feminine in Biblical Wisdom Literature: Selections Annotated & Explained
Translation & Annotation by Rabbi Rami Shapiro; Foreword by Rev. Cynthia Bourgeault, PhD
Uses the Hebrew books of Psalms, Proverbs, Song of Songs, Ecclesiastes and Job, Wisdom literature and the Wisdom of Solomon to clarify who Wisdom is. 5½ x 8½, 240 pp, Quality PB, 978-1-59473-109-9 **$16.99**

Ethics of the Sages: *Pirke Avot*—Annotated & Explained
Translation & Annotation by Rabbi Rami Shapiro Clarifies the ethical teachings of the early Rabbis.
5½ x 8½, 192 pp, Quality PB, 978-1-59473-207-2 **$16.99**

Hasidic Tales: Annotated & Explained: *Translation & Annotation by Rabbi Rami Shapiro*
Introduces the legendary tales of the impassioned Hasidic rabbis, presenting them as stories rather than as parables.
5½ x 8½, 240 pp, Quality PB, 978-1-893361-86-7 **$16.95**

The Hebrew Prophets: Selections Annotated & Explained
Translation & Annotation by Rabbi Rami Shapiro; Foreword by Zalman M. Schachter-Shalomi
Focuses on the central themes covered by all the Hebrew prophets. 5½ x 8½, 224 pp, Quality PB, 978-1-59473-037-5 **$16.99**

Zohar: Annotated & Explained *Translation & Annotation by Daniel C. Matt*
The best-selling author of *The Essential Kabbalah* brings together in one place the most important teachings of the Zohar, the canonical text of Jewish mystical tradition. 5½ x 8½, 176 pp, Quality PB, 978-1-893361-51-5 **$15.99**

EASTERN RELIGIONS

Bhagavad Gita: Annotated & Explained *Translation by Shri Purohit Swami*
Annotation by Kendra Crossen Burroughs Explains references and philosophical terms, shares the interpretations of famous spiritual leaders and scholars, and more. 5½ x 8½, 192 pp, Quality PB, 978-1-893361-28-7 **$16.95**

Dhammapada: Annotated & Explained *Translation by Max Müller and revised by Jack Maguire; Annotation by Jack Maguire* Contains all of Buddhism's key teachings. 5½ x 8½, 160 pp, b/w photos, Quality PB, 978-1-893361-42-3 **$14.95**

Rumi and Islam: Selections from His Stories, Poems, and Discourses—Annotated & Explained
Translation & Annotation by Ibrahim Gamard Focuses on Rumi's place within the Sufi tradition of Islam, providing insight into the mystical side of the religion. 5½ x 8½, 240 pp, Quality PB, 978-1-59473-002-3 **$15.99**

Selections from the Gospel of Sri Ramakrishna: Annotated & Explained
Translation by Swami Nikhilananda; Annotation by Kendra Crossen Burroughs
Introduces the fascinating world of the Indian mystic and the universal appeal of his message.
5½ x 8½, 240 pp, b/w photos, Quality PB, 978-1-893361-46-1 **$16.95**

Tao Te Ching: Annotated & Explained *Translation & Annotation by Derek Lin; Foreword by Lama Surya Das*
Introduces an Eastern classic in an accessible, poetic and completely original way.
5½ x 8½, 192 pp, Quality PB, 978-1-59473-204-1 **$16.99**

Spirituality & Crafts

The Knitting Way: A Guide to Spiritual Self-Discovery
by Linda Skolnik and Janice MacDaniels 7 x 9, 240 pp, Quality PB, 978-1-59473-079-5 **$16.99**

The Quilting Path: A Guide to Spiritual Discovery through Fabric, Thread and Kabbalah
by Louise Silk 7 x 9, 192 pp, Quality PB, 978-1-59473-206-5 **$16.99**

Spiritual Practice

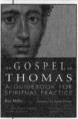

Divining the Body
Reclaim the Holiness of Your Physical Self *by Jan Phillips*
A practical and inspiring guidebook for connecting the body and soul in spiritual practice. Leads you into a milieu of reverence, mystery and delight, helping you discover your body as a pathway to the Divine.
8 x 8, 256 pp, Quality PB, 978-1-59473-080-1 **$16.99**

Finding Time for the Timeless: Spirituality in the Workweek
by John McQuiston II Simple, refreshing stories that provide you with examples of how you can refocus and enrich your daily life using prayer or meditation, ritual and other forms of spiritual practice.
5½ x 6¾, 208 pp, HC, 978-1-59473-035-1 **$17.99**

The Gospel of Thomas
A Guidebook for Spiritual Practice *by Ron Miller; Translations by Stevan Davies*
An innovative guide to bring a new spiritual classic into daily life.
6 x 9, 160 pp, Quality PB, 978-1-59473-047-4 **$14.99**

Earth, Water, Fire, and Air: Essential Ways of Connecting to Spirit
by Cait Johnson 6 x 9, 224 pp, HC, 978-1-893361-65-2 **$19.95**

Labyrinths from the Outside In: Walking to Spiritual Insight—A Beginner's Guide
by Donna Schaper and Carole Ann Camp
6 x 9, 208 pp, b/w illus. and photos, Quality PB, 978-1-893361-18-8 **$16.95**

Practicing the Sacred Art of Listening: A Guide to Enrich Your Relationships and Kindle Your Spiritual Life—The Listening Center Workshop
by Kay Lindahl 8 x 8, 176 pp, Quality PB, 978-1-893361-85-0 **$16.95**

Releasing the Creative Spirit: Unleash the Creativity in Your Life
by Dan Wakefield 7 x 10, 256 pp, Quality PB, 978-1-893361-36-2 **$16.95**

The Sacred Art of Bowing: Preparing to Practice
by Andi Young 5½ x 8½, 128 pp, b/w illus., Quality PB, 978-1-893361-82-9 **$14.95**

The Sacred Art of Chant: Preparing to Practice
by Ana Hernández 5½ x 8½, 192 pp, Quality PB, 978-1-59473-036-8 **$15.99**

The Sacred Art of Fasting: Preparing to Practice
by Thomas Ryan, CSP 5½ x 8½, 192 pp, Quality PB, 978-1-59473-078-8 **$15.99**

The Sacred Art of Forgiveness: Forgiving Ourselves and Others through God's Grace
by Marcia Ford 8 x 8, 176 pp, Quality PB, 978-1-59473-175-4 **$16.99**

The Sacred Art of Listening: Forty Reflections for Cultivating a Spiritual Practice
by Kay Lindahl; Illustrations by Amy Schnapper
8 x 8, 160 pp, b/w illus., Quality PB, 978-1-893361-44-7 **$16.99**

The Sacred Art of Lovingkindness: Preparing to Practice
by Rabbi Rami Shapiro; Foreword by Marcia Ford 5½ x 8½, 176 pp, Quality PB, 978-1-59473-151-8 **$16.99**

Sacred Speech: A Practical Guide for Keeping Spirit in Your Speech
by Rev. Donna Schaper 6 x 9, 176 pp, Quality PB, 978-1-59473-068-9 **$15.99**
HC, 978-1-893361-74-4 **$21.95**

Spirituality of the Seasons

Autumn: A Spiritual Biography of the Season   *Edited by Gary Schmidt and Susan M. Felch; Illustrations by Mary Azarian*
Rejoice in autumn as a time of preparation and reflection. Includes Wendell Berry, David James Duncan, Robert Frost, A. Bartlett Giamatti, E. B. White, P. D. James, Julian of Norwich, Garret Keizer, Tracy Kidder, Anne Lamott, May Sarton.
6 x 9, 320 pp, 5 b/w illus., Quality PB, 978-1-59473-118-1 **$18.99** HC, 978-1-59473-005-4 **$22.99**

Spring: A Spiritual Biography of the Season   *Edited by Gary Schmidt and Susan M. Felch; Illustrations by Mary Azarian*
Explore the gentle unfurling of spring and reflect on how nature celebrates rebirth and renewal. Includes Jane Kenyon, Lucy Larcom, Harry Thurston, Nathaniel Hawthorne, Noel Perrin, Annie Dillard, Martha Ballard, Barbara Kingsolver, Dorothy Wordsworth, Donald Hall, David Brill, Lionel Basney, Isak Dinesen, Paul Laurence Dunbar. 6 x 9, 352 pp, 6 b/w illus., HC, 978-1-59473-114-3 **$21.99**

Summer: A Spiritual Biography of the Season   *Edited by Gary Schmidt and Susan M. Felch; Illustrations by Barry Moser*
"A sumptuous banquet.... These selections lift up an exquisite wholeness found within an everyday sophistication."— ★ *Publishers Weekly* starred review
Includes Anne Lamott, Luci Shaw, Ray Bradbury, Richard Selzer, Thomas Lynch, Walt Whitman, Carl Sandburg, Sherman Alexie, Madeleine L'Engle, Jamaica Kincaid. 6 x 9, 304 pp, 5 b/w illus., HC, 978-1-59473-083-2 **$21.99**

Winter: A Spiritual Biography of the Season   *Edited by Gary Schmidt and Susan M. Felch; Illustrations by Barry Moser*
"This outstanding anthology features top-flight nature and spirituality writers on the fierce, inexorable season of winter.... Remarkably lively and warm, despite the icy subject." — ★ *Publishers Weekly* starred review.
Includes Will Campbell, Rachel Carson, Annie Dillard, Donald Hall, Ron Hansen, Jane Kenyon, Jamaica Kincaid, Barry Lopez, Kathleen Norris, John Updike, E. B. White.
6 x 9, 288 pp, 6 b/w illus., Deluxe PB w/flaps, 978-1-893361-92-8 **$18.95** HC, 978-1-893361-53-9 **$21.95**

Spirituality / Animal Companions

Blessing the Animals: Prayers and Ceremonies to Celebrate God's Creatures, Wild and Tame
Edited by Lynn L. Caruso 5 x 7¼, 256 pp, HC, 978-1-59473-145-7 **$19.99**

What Animals Can Teach Us about Spirituality: Inspiring Lessons from Wild and Tame Creatures
by Diana L. Guerrero 6 x 9, 176 pp, Quality PB, 978-1-893361-84-3 **$16.95**

Spirituality

Awakening the Spirit, Inspiring the Soul
30 Stories of Interspiritual Discovery in the Community of Faiths
Edited by Brother Wayne Teasdale and Martha Howard, MD; Foreword by Joan Borysenko, PhD
Thirty original spiritual mini-autobiographies showcase the varied ways that people come to faith—and what that means—in today's multi-religious world. 6 x 9, 224 pp, HC, 978-1-59473-039-9 **$21.99**

The Alphabet of Paradise: An A–Z of Spirituality for Everyday Life
by Howard Cooper 5 x 7¾, 224 pp, Quality PB, 978-1-893361-80-5 **$16.95**

Creating a Spiritual Retirement: A Guide to the Unseen Possibilities in Our Lives
by Molly Srode 6 x 9, 208 pp, b/w photos, Quality PB, 978-1-59473-050-4 **$14.99** HC, 978-1-893361-75-1 **$19.95**

Finding Hope: Cultivating God's Gift of a Hopeful Spirit
by Marcia Ford 8 x 8, 200 pp, Quality PB, 978-1-59473-211-9 **$16.99**

The Geography of Faith: Underground Conversations on Religious, Political and Social Change
by Daniel Berrigan and Robert Coles 6 x 9, 224 pp, Quality PB, 978-1-893361-40-9 **$16.95**

God Within: Our Spiritual Future—As Told by Today's New Adults
Edited by Jon M. Sweeney and the Editors at SkyLight Paths 6 x 9, 176 pp, Quality PB, 978-1-893361-15-7 **$14.95**

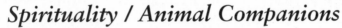

About SKYLIGHT PATHS Publishing

SkyLight Paths Publishing is creating a place where people of different spiritual traditions come together for challenge and inspiration, a place where we can help each other understand the mystery that lies at the heart of our existence.

Through spirituality, our religious beliefs are increasingly becoming a part of our lives—rather than *apart* from our lives. While many of us may be more interested than ever in spiritual growth, we may be less firmly planted in traditional religion. Yet, we do want to deepen our relationship to the sacred, to learn from our own as well as from other faith traditions, and to practice in new ways.

SkyLight Paths sees both believers and seekers as a community that increasingly transcends traditional boundaries of religion and denomination—people wanting to learn from each other, *walking together, finding the way.*

For your information and convenience, at the back of this book we have provided a list of other SkyLight Paths books you might find interesting and useful. They cover the following subjects:

Buddhism / Zen	Hinduism /	Mysticism
Catholicism	Vedanta	Poetry
Children's Books	Inspiration	Prayer
Christianity	Islam / Sufism	Religious Etiquette
Comparative Religion	Judaism / Kabbalah /	Retirement
Current Events	Enneagram	Spiritual Biography
Earth-Based Spirituality	Meditation	Spiritual Direction
Global Spiritual	Midrash Fiction	Spirituality
Perspectives	Monasticism	Women's Interest
Gnosticism		Worship

Or phone, fax, mail or e-mail to: SKYLIGHT PATHS Publishing
Sunset Farm Offices, Route 4 • P.O. Box 237 • Woodstock, Vermont 05091
Tel: (802) 457-4000 • Fax: (802) 457-4004 • www.skylightpaths.com
Credit card orders: (800) 962-4544 (8:30AM–5:30PM ET Monday–Friday)
Generous discounts on quantity orders. SATISFACTION GUARANTEED. Prices subject to change.